D0859424

Quality Management In Financial Services

by Charles A. Aubrey, II

Hitchcock Publishing Company
Hitchcock Building
Wheaton, IL 60188

To my wife Elizabeth and
my children Chuckie, Faith,
Hope and Joy.

ISBN 0-933931-02-6

1st Printing, April, 1985
2nd Printing, June, 1988
©1985 by Hitchcock Publishing Co.

All rights reserved. No part of this book may be reproduced in any
form without written permission from Hitchcock Publishing Company.

Publisher: Hitchcock Publishing Company
Hitchcock Building
Wheaton, IL 60188

THE AUTHOR

Charles A. Aubrey II is Chief Quality Officer and Manager of Quality and Productivity Improvement at BANC ONE CORPORATION, Columbus, Ohio.

He previously held vice presidential positions at Continental Illinois National Bank and Citizens National Bank. He has held positions as personnel director, lending officer, controller, operations officer, and customer service manager.

Mr. Aubrey has been a lecturer at both DePaul University and Loyola University in Chicago. He taught in the management department and communications department respectively.

A commander in the U.S. Navy Reserve, he has served for over 22 years on numerous ships and shore assignments and holds specialties in propulsion, industrial and quality control engineering, shipping control, communications, personnel, management and administration.

Mr. Aubrey holds a BA from Lewis University, an MBA from DePaul University and has done additional study at Harvard and at the University of Illinois. This book represents a portion of his thesis for a DBA.

The author lectures and has written and delivered numerous papers, many of which are listed in the bibliography. He is also the co-author of *Management by Participation—Involving People in Quality and Productivity,* 1987, UNIPUB/Kraus Thompson, and has co-authored and co-produced a film of the same title.

CONTENTS

IV

VII. SAMPLE SURVEYS AND PERCEPTION RESULTS

FOREWORD

Quality control as a well-developed body of theory and techniques has existed for a long time in product manufacturing industries. It is only relatively recently that financial institutions, along with other service industries, have begun to flirt with the formal application of quality control along the lines defined by the manufacturing model.

There are a couple of reasons for this. First, are the obvious dissimilarities between the processes of producing physical products and handling financial transactions which complicate the wholesale use of quality control tools in banking. Secondly, the basic nature of the banking business, with its pervasive tradition of responsibility in handling other people's money, always requires extensive controls which inherently tend to yield high quality.

Still, any organized attempt to develop a program to enhance quality in a bank will inevitably take on some of the characteristics of classical "quality control" including the formal structure of the quality control unit itself, as well as activities such as setting quality standards, measuring conformance to standards, and reporting to management.

Before going any further, it would be useful to define what we mean by quality. Frequently, the term expresses a general, almost abstract characteristic of excellence; it evokes the sense of an intangible, immeasurable attribute. (So when a business analyst slips into the jargon of his trade and says something is qualitative rather than quantitative, he is suggesting it is less concrete, less susceptible to measurement.) Since the heart of a meaningful quality program has to be an effective system for measuring quality, our definition of quality should be rooted in measurable terms. A recent National Science Foundation study developed an approach to measuring quality in banks. The study articulated a definition of quality which expresses its essence aptly:

> *"Quality is conformance to standards which represent the product or service's basic characteristics and are based upon customer needs and expectations."*

What this means is that customer needs and expectations need to be determined regarding each product and service. These needs then should be reflected in standards—quality standards which are simply the product or service's basic characteristics. Lastly, the product or service should continuously conform to the standards and if it does, customers will be satisfied and continue to buy the product or service.

To carry out quality management a system must be established to set standards or objectives, monitor the standards or give feedback and be able to influence the system or make changes when the standards are not met. A model of a quality management system for a financial institution is illustrated on the following page. This model is not limited to strictly "banking" type activities. Many larger financial institutions have applied or carried out some or all of the activities in other service activities they perform for themselves. Applications have been made in food service, physical security, printing and graphic services, insurance, shipping and receiving and mail handling as well as accounting, computer operation and automated system development and programming.

If nothing else, quality management for financial services are good management techniques. These techniques assure that high quality financial services, as defined by the customer, are delivered continuously and constantly. If not, then they are an early warning system to quickly focus management attention to a poor quality situation before it becomes a quality problem.

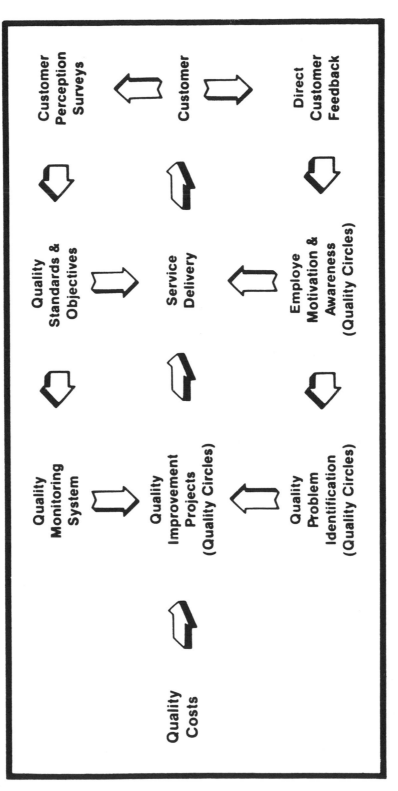

QUALITY CONTROL SYSTEM

Quality Costs

Quality Monitoring System

Quality Improvement Projects (Quality Circles)

Quality Problem Identification (Quality Circles)

Quality Standards & Objectives

Service Delivery

Employe Motivation & Awareness (Quality Circles)

Customer Perception Surveys

Customer

Direct Customer Feedback

Quality is conformance to standards
which represent the product or
service's basic characteristics and are
based upon customer needs and
expectations.

CHAPTER I

Determining Your Quality
Commitment and Developing a Plan

To help establish conceptual footing and a plan an organization must determine the level of quality commitment. Several weeks of meetings with management, staff, and sales people in various departments are needed to get a feeling for the current climate relative to quality in a bank.

Particular attention should be focused on perceptions of what quality is and what special activities are currently being pursued to measure, sustain, and improve quality. A sample of senior and middle line, and staff people in both sales and operations should be surveyed. The following interview questions can provide a degree of structure in the discussions.

INTERVIEW QUESTIONS:

1. During this year's planning process, were formal objectives regarding service quality prepared?
2. Have these objectives been met? If so, how has this been determined?
3. Do you intend to make any changes during the remainder of the year which will improve service quality performance?
4. Do you intend to incorporate quality objectives in next year's plan? If so, have you formulated any of these yet?
5. Do you have formalized service quality policies and procedures written and implemented?
6. What specific standards do you actually use to evaluate your current service quality performance?
7. Do you have a method or system to apply the standards? If so, are you satisfied with the results?
8. Do you generate a quality performance report(s) on a periodic basis comparing actual quality performance against your standards?
9. Do you have quality control mechanisms in effect to provide feedback to those areas which have made errors? If yes, how does the system work?
10. Do you communicate your quality performance to your seniors? If so, through what media and to what extent?
11. Are you aware of departmental or corporate standards used to measure your service quality performance?

12. Do you feel top management is committed to high quality? Does this help or hurt your efforts toward quality performance?
13. What can and should be done to increase commitment to quality assurance at all levels?
14. Do you have any suggestions or guidelines which should be incorporated into a corporate policies bulletin on service quality?
15. What would you estimate to be the current cost of quality assurance within your area? In other words, what percent of your total expenses and total manpower is associated with quality control and error correction?
16. Are your current resources limiting your level of quality? Do you require additional expense or personnel to improve your level of service quality performance to a higher level than what your performance is currently? If yes, how many more personnel would you require and what additional expenses would you incur?
17. In your opinion, what is the relationship between quality and productivity?
18. Do you feel your customers perceive the same relationship?
19. What is your perception of what our customers think about our service quality performance and employee awareness of the importance of the customer?
20. In your opinion, do you think our employees have an appropriate customer awareness or sensitivity attitude? If no, why not and what can be done to improve this attitude?
21. Do your training programs include customer sensitivity or awareness training? If so, how is this being accomplished?

OPERATING MANAGEMENT PERCEPTIONS AND PRACTICES

What follows is a summary of oral responses provided by management people who offered comments on what their units are doing to assure quality and their observations about quality in general. These are typical responses in most financial institutions.

Performance Measures

Most operating units capture some data on performance which affects quality. Some common measures are number of errors, holdover, and turnaround time. (Chapter 2 displays various types of data which, according to the respondents, is collected in their respective units.)

Performance Quality Objectives

While the majority of managers affirmed the existence of objectives relating to quality—and asserted that they were being met—there seemed to be a generally low level of awareness of just what the objectives were. The responses indicated a lack of regular reports comparing actual to standard performance along quality dimensions and, where such reports existed, they seldom got visibility above the division manager level but stayed within the unit of origin.

None of the respondents indicated a knowledge of department or coporate quality objectives, though there was a universal feeling that senior management is committed to high quality.

SURVEY RESULTS

- Some quality data is captured—few standards
- Quality objectives are set and met—low level of awareness
- Quality is perceived to be at a high level—room for improvement

Attitudes Toward Quality

Most of the people interviewed believed that their unit's quality was very good. There was general agreement that improvement in quality would be initiated most effectively by increased emphasis on quality by the corporate office and department heads, with continual reinforcement up and down the line at all levels.

The one area of weakness in performance which was widely recognized was in the level of customer relations skills exhibited by the work force generally. The pervasive view was that employees do not display adequate sensitivity to customers. The solutions posed most often were better training, continuous efforts to promote awareness, and managerial attention. Very few units, according to the respondents, have formal training in customer service skills, including human relations training or awareness programs.

Recurring Comments

A number of comments surfaced repeatedly in discussions with operating management and staff. Here is a sampling:

1. The bank needs a centralized inquiry and complaint tracking system to monitor problems by: type or information requested, type of problem, customer, and product.
2. Automated systems support is critical to maintaining high quality.
3. The quality of the workforce is deteriorating with obvious implications for overall quality.
4. Supervisory training should emphasize quality along with the other aspects of production.
5. Customer service personnel too frequently are assigned based on technical knowledge rather than interpersonal skills.
6. The performance appraisal process should provide for evaluation of the quality aspects of performance and this should be reflected in the reward system.
7. Communication between units needs to be improved.
8. Sales people need to be thoroughly trained in all aspects of products and services and understand operation constraints which limit what they can reasonably offer customers.
9. Apply better means of assessing customer perceptions of service.

10. Pay particular attention to new accounts which are particularly vulnerable to quality problems.
11. The impact of poor quality on customers is especially critical today in view of the increasing assertiveness of customers.

ADMINISTRATIVE PERCEPTIONS OF QUALITY

A number of interviews were conducted with key administrative or sales people in each line department to get a flavor of how administrators view quality. Since the quality of services is a vital part of their marketability, it is important that quality be high and that sales people have confidence in that quality. Interviews with select administrators suggest that there is considerable perceived room for improvement.

Although respondents generally view the quality of the sales force as very good, some commented that with rapid staff growth to accommodate business expansion, they had experienced a temporary dilution in experience.

The activity that came in for the sharpest criticism was the operating support provided to commercial services. Errors and lack of timeliness in service delivery and response were cited as the chief lapses in quality. The most frequent complaint made by the respondents was that errors occurred too frequently and took too long to correct. There was a general feeling that customers would tolerate errors if they were corrected promptly. However, this kind of response to problems was believed to be untypical.

It was felt that because of inadequate communication processes, improper information, or faulty procedures, it is difficult to get customer problems to the right area for handling. Further, because of the frequent impact of multiple units on particular transactions, there are sometimes jurisdictional delays during which no one area or person will assume responsibility for fixing a problem. Even when the problem is ultimately resolved, the quality of the final communication with the customer is not uniform or reliable.

The fundamental problem is perceived to be a lack of sensitivity to the customer's needs, an absence of customer awareness.

CUSTOMER PERCEPTIONS OF QUALITY

Although the perceptions of quality held by operating management and administrative people offer a vital perspective, the most important set of perceptions is that held by customers and potential customers. There is no comprehensive study available which tells how bank customers perceive quality. Research among select groups of customers and potential customers can include, among other data, findings relating to quality. The most notable examples are the annual studies done by Greenwich Research Associates concentrating on Corporate and Correspondent Banking.

The Greenwich studies contain a great deal of data without attempting to make an overall ranking of banks by significant characteristics. To get a feeling for a particular characteristic such as service quality, numerous questions which relate to service quality must be reviewed.

Corporate executives evaluate banks on their ability to meet their needs by the flexibility of service (credit and non-credit) provided (#1), the quality of the account officers (#2), and the strength of the banks interest in their company (#3). The strength of the banks operating capabilities is ranked #9. Executives cite the reasons that banks become more important to them is the amount of domestic credit provided (#1), the level of cash management services (#2), and the caliber of account officers (#3). On the other hand, banks become less important due to lack of account officer attention (#1), too many operating errors (#2), and below average caliber of account officers (#3).

As can be generally observed the scope and depth of services offered by a bank are the prime considerations of corporate executives in choosing, continuing and enhancing bank relationships, with account officer capabilities second. The decision to reduce or discontinue bank relationships is generally based on the lack of account officer capabilities, weaknesses in bank operations or high error rates.

The quality characteristics of an account officer include timeliness of response, performance, experience, knowledge and time assigned to an account. Operating quality includes speed and accuracy of the service and speed of error correction.

Correspondent bankers evaluate and select banks similarly to corporate executives; the top three criteria are the same: flexibility of services to meet needs, the caliber of account officers and the bank's interest in the correspondent. Operating capabilities, which were ranked ninth by corporate executives are ranked fifth by bank executives. Once a bank is corresponding, the relationship is evaluated in terms of accuracy of the services (#1), quality of cash letter services (#2), and flexibility of services (#3). Correspondent banks become more important and are utilized more due to fast cash letter services (#1), more account officer attention (#2), and more overline support (#3). They become less important and service is discontinued due to inadequate service from calling officers (#1), decline in the need for correspondent services (#2), and too many operational errors (#3).

Although the scope and depth of services and the caliber of account officers are most important in the evaluation and selection of a correspondent, operating quality, accuracy and speed are the major factors used to determine whether to continue and increase service usage. Account officer attention and service usage and flexibility are of less importance than operating quality once a correspondent is selected. Bankers are also more sensitive to quality in services than to the price they pay for those services.

Another example of research which yields data on quality are the "shopping" studies. These studies utilize "shopping" by trained researchers posing as customers and documenting their perceptions of products and services with particular attention paid to the customer relations skills of personal bankers, tellers, and receptionists. Performance is then compared with the results of similar studies at other banks and past study results.

The Greenwich research and "shopping" studies are only two examples of a variety of surveys which are periodically done to measure customer and non-customer perceptions of financial services. It is clear that quality is a vital dimension of how customers and potential customers evaluate banks, so enhancing your position in the marketplace demands continued and increased attention to quality.

SUMMARY CHART OF QUALITY ACTIVITIES
(PRIOR TO IMPLEMENTING A FORMAL PROGRAM)

Division/Unit	PROCESSING QUALITY: Quality Performance Reports	Errors #	Errors & Adjustments $	Holdover #	Holdover $	Turnaround Time	Systems Downtime	Customer Profile	Quality Surveys	Rates of Quality	Standards for Quality	CUSTOMER SERVICE QUALITY: Customer Service Reports	Investigations & Inquiries	Investigations vs. Inquiries	Aging	Errors	Holdover	Customer Service Section
BOND																		
Bond Operations	X		X									X	X		X		X	X
COMMERCIAL SERVICES																		
International Services	X	X	X						X			X	X	X	X			X
Collections	X	X	X									X	X	X				X
Credit Information	X			X		X												
Paying & Receiving	X		X				X		X	X		X	X	X		X		
Precious Metals																		
Customer Service	X		X															
Signature	X			X								X	X		X			
Letters of Credit	X		X	X	X		X					X	X	X	X	X	X	X
Loan Support/Processing	X	X		X	X				X			X	X	X	X	X	X	X
Loan Review	X	X				X	X		X	X								
Domestic Wire Transfer	X	X	X							X		X	X	X	X	X	X	X
Support Services	X		X			X		X										
Safekeeping/Special Services												X	X	X	X	X	X	
FX Operations												X	X		X	X	X	
PERSONAL BANKING																		
Facilities Operations	X	X	X	X		X		X	X			X	X		X			X
Charge Card Operations												X	X		X			X
Consumer Credit Operations												X	X		X			
Mortgage Servicing												X	X		X			

SUMMARY CHART OF QUALITY ACTIVITIES
(PRIOR TO IMPLEMENTING A FORMAL PROGRAM)

Division/Unit	PROCESSING QUALITY											CUSTOMER SERVICE QUALITY						
	Quality Performance Reports	Errors #	Errors & Adjustments $	Holdover #	Holdover $	Turnaround Time	Systems Downtime	Customer Profile	Quality Surveys	Rates of Quality	Standards for Quality	Customer Service Reports	Investigations & Inquiries	Investigations vs. Inquiries	Aging	Errors	Holdover	Customer Service Section
REAL ESTATE																		
Real Estate Operations												X	X		X			
TRUST																		
Trust Operations	X	X				X	X			X		X	X	X				X
CHECK PROCESSING																		
Balance Control	X	X	X	X	X			X				X	X	X	X	X	X	
Bookkeeping	X	X	X	X	X			X		X								
Document Processing	X	X	X	X	X			X		X								
Proof Transit	X	X	X	X	X			X		X	X							
Remittance Banking	X	X						X		X	X	X	X			X	X	
GENERAL SERVICES																		
Properties Development						X												
Properties Management								X					X					
General Duties								X	X	X			X					
Distribution Services								X	X	X								
Printing and Graphic	X	X																
Services	X		X					X	X	X								
Records Management/ Storage/Filing	X	X								X	X							
SYSTEMS																		
Systems Development	X					X	X		X	X	X							
Systems Operations	X	X				X	X	X	X	X	X							

A QUALITY ASSURANCE PROGRAM

While there should be justifiable pride among your staff members in the bank's overall quality, there also should be a general recognition that they can do better. What's needed is to generate a more visible, emphatic commitment to quality at all levels of management. This commitment should be embodied in demanding objectives and reinforced in a reward system. It should be made unequivocably clear to all employees that quality really matters. Finally, increase an awareness of the customer throughout your staff and polish customer relations skills of sales and service people.

A unit should be formed to provide a focal point for the corporation's efforts to maintain and enhance quality. A Quality Assurance Division will fulfill this mission in a cooperative effort with management by pursuing these objectives:

Mission

It is the mission of the Quality Assurance Division to assist management at all levels throughout the corporation to maintain a consistently high quality of service in all activities and assist in creating and maintaining an appropriate awareness on the part of every employee of the importance of quality and the customer.

Quality assurance objectives

Objective 1 Develop, organize, and staff the Quality Assurance Division.

Objective 2 Help management of various units establish or update quality assurance objectives, policies, procedures, and performance standards.

Objective 3 Develop, then help management implement, a comprehensive quality control, monitoring, and reporting system.

Objective 4 Develop and implement a quality cost measurement system.

Objective 5 Develop and implement a communications and motivational program to enhance employee awareness of the importance of the customer and to ensure a high quality of customer service throughout the corporation. (Quality Circles)

Objective 6 Design and employ customer feedback programs to measure customer perceptions of service and product quality.

Objective 7 Continually review quality assurance and customer awareness programs and trends in banking and other service industries.

MISSION

It is the mission of the Quality Assurance Division to assist management at all levels throughout the corporation to maintain a consistently high quality of service in all our activities and assist in creating and maintaining an appropriate awareness on the part of every employee of the importance of quality and the customer.

CHAPTER II

Quality Standards and Measures

Quality characteristics or standards and their corresponding measures should be developed during new product development, but in most financial institutions they will already be delivering hundreds of mature products which have already gone through the new product development stage. Therefore, it will be necessary to develop quality characteristics or standards and their corresponding measures for the hundreds of mature products that are already being delivered to customers. This will be the most significant task in most institutions. After these are established, the task will then be to shift to the process as it relates to new product development.

In the financial service industry, which is very labor-intensive, the process for developing quality characteristics for products and service should be done through a group participative process. The people processing the product know the product best and know the problems that can occur and where they can occur. The approach that has worked in numerous financial institutions is a series of four two-hour group meetings which take place with those people under a first line supervisor. Either all the people may be involved under the first line supervisor or the supervisor and selected key people. This participatory group process takes approximately eight hours of time for each section under a supervisor and approximately an additional and equal number of hours for the quality control analyst or engineer, who will facilitate the process, outside of the eight hours of meetings.

QUALITY AWARENESS AND UNDERSTANDING

The first of the four two-hour sessions is devoted to defining quality, to discussing what quality is, how it can be measured, the benefits of measuring quality, how quality once it is measured can be analyzed and, therefore, controlled and improved. The second part of this session is devoted to developing functional flowcharts for each distinct product that is being processed by the section. It is not unusual to have anywhere from one to six products being provided by an individual section. In most cases they are not providing the total processing of a product but only part of the process to deliver that service. The flowcharts start with all sources of input to the section and they identify all the major functions or changes of state which take place during the processing. They end with the identification of where each finished service goes, be it to the customer or to another area of the bank. These flow charts are thoroughly discussed so that all members understand the charts and the process they represent.

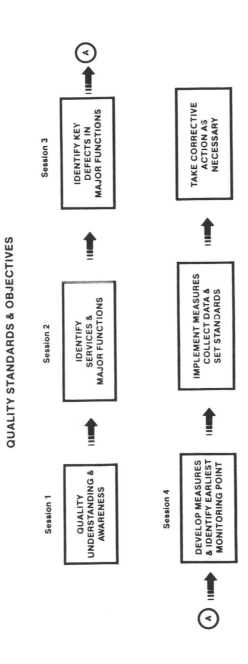

QUALITY STANDARDS & OBJECTIVES

Session 1

QUALITY
UNDERSTANDING &
AWARENESS

Session 2

IDENTIFY
SERVICES &
MAJOR FUNCTIONS

Session 3

IDENTIFY KEY
DEFECTS IN
MAJOR FUNCTIONS

Ⓐ

Session 4

DEVELOP MEASURES
& IDENTIFY EARLIEST
MONITORING POINT

Ⓐ

IMPLEMENT MEASURES
COLLECT DATA &
SET STANDARDS

TAKE CORRECTIVE
ACTION AS
NECESSARY

At the conclusion of the first session each member is given a copy of the functional flowcharts that were developed and the concept of a deviation is explained. A deviation is anything that goes wrong in the process. The flowchart is like a blueprint diagram. If everything goes right, and the service has matched the blueprint, then the service is delivered correctly, but when something deviates from this blueprint, it is called a deviation. The individuals in the group are then charged or given a homework assignment to develop all of the deviations that could possibly take place in the functional flowchart. It's important to note here that they're not asked to identify the deviations that *do* take place, but those that do take place as well as those that *could* take place during the process.

BRAINSTORMING THE PROCESS

Ideally, the next two-hour meeting is scheduled for the following day. Depending on the work load and the scheduling for the area in which the process is taking place, the process sometimes may take place every other day, one two-hour meeting a week in successive weeks, but it has been proven that the closer the meetings can be to each other, the better the results of the process. In the second meeting the people come back together in the group, having individually generated a list of all the deviations which they believe can go wrong in the process. The second session then starts out with a controlled brainstorming method in which each person responds in turn one at a time going clockwise or counterclockwise around the table identifying one deviation which they have identified. This process may take place and continue for 15 to 20 minutes at which point a break should be taken for people to collect their thoughts, to rest, possibly think about and jot down some new ideas on deviations.

While the process is taking place and the people are in turn giving their possible deviations, a person is recording these on a flipchart and they are numbered. When the flowchart was completed in the previous session, each of the functions as well as the input and the output points were given unique numbers so that when deviations were identified, the person who identified the deviation also made an attempt at indicating at what point on the flowchart that deviation was introduced into the system or where it took place. It is not unusual for this controlled brainstorming to take up the entire two hours and in some cases an extension of an hour or sometimes infrequently two hours is needed to thoroughly complete the brainstorming of all possible deviations.

At this point, the participants are given the list of defects to take home with them and review. They are specifically charged with reviewing the list, to determine whether there are duplicates, to assure that they understand each of the deviations and to be sure that there are no additional deviations which have not been identified which need to be recorded. The next day when they return this list will be discussed.

SELECTING THE KEY DEFECTS

The third session, which is hopefully the following day, begins with a discussion of

FLOW CHART

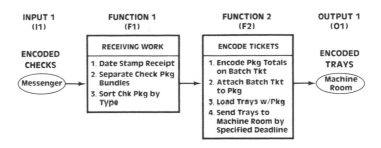

INPUT 1 (I1)	FUNCTION 1 (F1)	FUNCTION 2 (F2)	OUTPUT 1 (O1)

ENCODED
CHECKS
 	
(Messenger)
	RECEIVING WORK
	1. Date Stamp Receipt
	2. Separate Check Pkg
	   Bundles
	3. Sort Chk Pkg by
	   Type
		ENCODE TICKETS
		1. Encode Pkg Totals
		   on Batch Tkt
		2. Attach Batch Tkt
		   to Pkg
		3. Load Trays w/Pkg
		4. Send Trays to
		   Machine Room by
		   Specified Deadline
			ENCODED
			TRAYS
			
			Machine
			Room

A completed flow chart is a graphic representation of the sequence of events in any process. It gives a step-by-step detailed record of the order in which work is done to facilitate analysis.

the list of deviations which have been identified on the previous day. The group, in a discussion format, will combine like deviations, will add any new deviations and discuss those that anyone has any doubts about. At this point the goal is a complete list that is concise, accurate and understandable.

Next, the group is asked to rank or vote on those deviations which are key quality determinates. Key quality determinates are those deviations which meet one of two tests. The first test is: does it impact the customer significantly if it takes place? The second test is: if it happens does it consume a large amount of resources to correct or make right? For example, it may take a relatively high proportion of time to reprocess or an interest penalty may be incurred if a transaction is not handled properly.

The voting process consists of 15 cards handed out to each member. Each member then reviews the list of deviations and selects the 15 which they feel, based on the two tests, are most key. The second step is then to rank them from 1 to 15; a weight of 15 being the most important, a ranking of one being the least important. The cards are collected and compiled in a matter of minutes. The deviations which have received votes then are ranked from highest weight to lowest weight. These then reflect the groups concensus as to the key deviations. The key deviations are those for which quality measures and quality standards will be developed. All quality deviations identified are not measured, but only the key ones. If you were to try to monitor and measure several hundred items in each area the reporting and inspection process would be unwieldy and you would in fact be making everything important, and if everything is important nothing is important. Therefore, only concentrate on the key deviations.

At the end of this session the group is introduced to the concept of measurement. Most measures take the form of a ratio or the number of deviations which could occur that have been identified divided by the volume processed. These ratios are called quality measures. A second method that is used less often is called a frequency. A frequency is simply the number of occurrences that took place or the number of deviations that happened during a specific time period—a week, a month, a day, etc. So in effect they are implicitly a ratio, the number of deviations over a time period whether it be days, weeks or months. This type of quality measure is discouraged but is useful in some situations. It's important to note here that our goal is to take deviations and convert them into measures. At this point we no longer use the term deviation, which was indicative of something going wrong in the process. We now call them defects. We call them defects because when we began measuring their occurrence, they will be quality standards which will not be met and, therefore, classified as a defect. After the group has been introduced to the concept of measurement a list of the key deviations in descending order is given to them and they are charged with developing measures for these items for the following session, which hopefully will take place on the following day.

DEVELOPING QUALITY MEASURES

The fourth session begins with a group using the controlled brainstorming technique of listing all of the measures which they have developed for all of the defects. This process continues with a break every 15 to 20 minutes until all possible measures have been exhausted for the list of key deviations. At the conclusion of the listing process, discussion takes place so everyone understands each of the measures that have been identified, and that there are measures for every one of the key defects, to make sure there are no duplicates, and, wherever appropriate, if additional measures can be generated those are added to the list.

The last step in the measurement process is to vote on measures when there are more than one possible measure for each defect that has been identified. If there is more than one measure, the group votes on which measure they feel, simply by raising hands, with each person having one vote, which is the most effective measure for that defect. The last thing accomplished in this session is to go back to the functional flowchart which was developed in the first session and indicate where in the flow chart is the earliest point that each measure can be implemented. The objective is to identify the earliest point in the process that each defect can be identified and fixed so that it can be caught as early as possible in the process. For example, if a defect occurs in the first step or function of the process, it would be most desirable to be able to catch it in the second step or before the second step rather than catch it in the tenth step or the tenth function. If you catch it in the tenth step you may have to go back and redo steps 1 through 9 before preceeding to step 10. If you can catch it at or before the second step, then there would be a minimum of reprocessing and less possibility that the defect would escape to the customer.

The next step in the process is to take the total list of defects, the flowchart, the key defects and the measures and present them to the area management. The quality control analyst or engineer along with the supervisor presents these items to the next level of management for their modification, additions and approval. Upon approval by the appropriate level of management the measures are then implemented. It is

QUALITY MEASURE DEVELOPMENT

DEFECT: Ticket not attached to package

MEASURE: $$\frac{\text{Packages Without Tickets}}{\text{Total Packages Processed}}$$

DEFECT: Trays Submitted Past Deadline

MEASURE: Trays Submitted Past Deadline
and/or
$$\frac{\text{Trays Submitted Past Deadline}}{\text{Trays Submitted}}$$

now the responsibility of the quality control engineer or analyst working with the supervisor to implement the measures that have been approved in the appropriate point in the process. The flowchart which was used to identify the earliest point in the process is used as a starting point but the analyst together with the supervisor assess whether that, in fact, is the earliest point in the process or if an earlier point can be established. It is also the responsibility of the quality control analyst to assess the best way to collect data. The possibilities range from collecting data through automation which may or may not be in place all the way to manual sampling. The analyst designs check sheets, reporting forms, sampling plans and works to coordinate automation as necessary to most efficiently and effectively gather the data needed for the measures.

DETERMINING QUALITY MEASURES

- Identify the quality control unit
- Identify services (items of output)
- Identify functions performed
- Identify probable quality deviations
- Select key quality deviations
- Identify earliest monitoring points for deviations
- Implement monitoring

QUALITY STANDARDS

Once the measures have been implemented, monitoring (100% or sampling) begins. Several days to weeks of data are collected depending on the amount of volume and closely monitored by the supervisor and analyst. This is to assure understanding on the part of those operators and inspectors who are collecting and reporting. Control charts are constructed to determine the process capability of the system. The mean quality level for each measure and either one and two standard deviation points, once determined, are considered the system's process capabilities.

The process capability is now the basis for setting the quality standard or objective for each measure. This process tells empirically what the quality level is but more importantly you need to know how your customers feel about the quality level of the service they are receiving. The methods of receiving input from customers are various and range from very simple to complex. These methods will be discussed later in Chapter VI but are an important ingredient in determining the standards.

Let us suppose that a process has the capability of .005% of checks misfiled. Most managers would agree that five checks misfiled out of 100,000 is reasonable for their operation or from a consumer point of view. However when actually surveyed, consumers expected even better quality. If customer expectations are close to the process capability then a goal or objective could be set slightly better than the process capability to motivate better performance and assure customer satisfaction. If customer expectations are much greater than the process capability then several avenues are possible. A breakthrough or quality improvement project could be initiated to dramatically improve the quality level. You could continue at the same quality level with a significantly increased standard and possibly motivate improvement but more likely not, and lose customers.

On the other extreme, a checking account statement delivery process could have a process capability of delivery 10 working days after cutoff. This, many managers and consumers would agree, sounds too long. Survey data, however, revealed that this is an adequate quality level for customers. Therefore, it would have been imprudent to waste resources to improve the quality level further.

It is important from a motivational standpoint that standards are both challenging as well as achievable. If they are not doable, employees will give up. If they do not allow the employee to stretch, then their potential will be minimized.

As can be seen the customers expectations and needs are extremely important in setting quality standards in mature financial services.

MEASURING QUALITY AND SETTING QUALITY STANDARDS FOR NEW SERVICES

This is a more difficult task but takes the same form as for mature products. Once the need for a new product has been determined and this should include extensive market research rich with potential customer surveys, the marketing, operating, quality and product management people together write the service characteristics or quality specifications. Operations and quality control then identify the existing

	Defect 1	Defect 2			Data Collection Log					
MON	I									
TUES	I	II								
WED										
THU	III	I								
FRI		I								

WHAT CRITERIA ARE REPORTED?

- **Accuracy of Output**
- **Distribution of Output**
- **Timeliness of Output**
- **Quality of Output**
- **On-Line Availability**
- **Response Time**
- **Systems Development Schedules**
- **Response to Problems**
- **Attitude & Cooperativeness**

processes that will provide the service, and model or engineer the new process that will have to be created, and their prospective quality level. If the process capability is adequate or at least close to the specifications, the new service should go ahead and the existing quality standards used to launch the service. If the process capability is far apart, a breakthrough or quality improvement project will be necessary prior to launch. If the specifications and process capability are far apart and a breakthrough seems unlikely or there are no resources to carry out an improvement project, then the new service should not be introduced.

QUALITY CONTROL MONITORING SYSTEM

Defect/Control Subject	This Month's Defect Ratio	This Month's Defect %
Misfiled Checks/Checks Filed	1062/21673	.049
Missing Checks/Checks Sent to Customers	16/16079	.001

Last Month's Defect %	Month Previous Defect %	Standard	QCI Unweighed	Weight	QCI Weighed	Proc. Cap. UCL/LCL
.072	.163*	.055	112%	2	224	.092/.030
.002	.004	.002	200%	1	200	.004/.0007
					424	QCI Points
					3	Weights
					141%	QCI

*Process out of control (outside process capability)

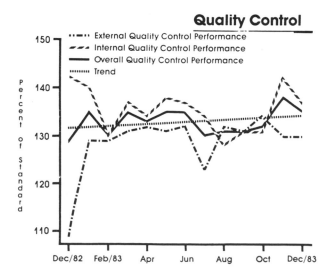

Quality Control

- External Quality Control Performance
- Internal Quality Control Performance
- Overall Quality Control Performance
- Trend

Percent of standard

150 — 140 — 130 — 120 — 110

Dec/82 Feb/83 Apr Jun Aug Oct Dec/83

Bookkeeping Services

Defect/Control Subject	This Period's Defect Ratio	This Period's Defect %	Last Month's Defect %	Previous Month's Defect %	Standard	Process Capability UCL/LCL	QCI% Unweighted	Weight	QCI% Weighted
Wrong Account Number/Total Deposits	76/37,936	.2	.3	.1	.1	.4/.08	50		
Non-Endorsed Deposits/Total Deposits	113/37,936	.3	.2	.1	.3	.4/.1	100		
Input Quality									
Missing Items/Total Statements	60/49,538	.12*	.08	.09	.08	.1/.05	67	6	402
Stop Payment Incorrect/Total Stop Payments	6/2,376	.25	.23	.21	.26	.28/.02	104	5	520
Misfiled Items/Total Checks & Debits	24/236,799	.01	.03	.04	.01	.04/.007	100	4	400
								(15)	1,322
Internal Quality Performance									88%
Wrong Statement Sent/Total Statements	14/49,538	.03	.03	.04	.02	.06/.01	67	4	268
Missing Items/Total Statements	4/49,538	.008*	.005	.002	.004	.006/.001	50	3	150
Incorrect Adjustment/Total Statements	33/49,538	.07	.08	.07	.06	.09/.05	86	5	430
								(12)	848
External Quality Performance									71%
								(27)	2,170
Overall Quality Performance									80%

*Out of control

19

EXAMPLES OF QUALITY MEASURES AND OBJECTIVES

A service characteristic of commercial credit (borrowing money) which is very high on a financial service customer's list of importance is the amount of credit they receive. A measurement of this service characteristic could be the percent of credit received over or divided by the credit requests. Specific objectives or standards for this quality measure could be 100% for customers who consider the bank their lead or first tier bank, 90% for second tier or 80% for third tier. Not supplying adequate credit to customers who consider the bank as their primary lender (assuming credit worthiness) could cause these customers to develop new bank relationships and lead to a loss of both current and future business. Not attempting to supply increased credit to customers for which you are a second or third tier bank would effectively keep you from becoming their primary bank. On the other hand, if resources are limited you may want to design your objectives or standards to keep your position stable if you have an appropriate customer mix and are profitable.

In an operating area a service characteristic of a checking account (demand deposit) is deposit credits. A quality measure for the deposit characteristic could be the number of misposted deposits over or divided by the total number of deposits posted. A specific standard would be one for every 3,000 deposits. If this ratio is not met or exceeded customers could become dissatisfied with the service and switch banks. Each misposted deposit could result in an investigation and possible compensation to the customer for his loss of use of funds. If this ratio is not met it would signal management of a problem and an effort would be launched to discover the cause of the excessive quality deviations.

A third example is the customer service or investigation process. An important characteristic of this function, since it is usually a result of a quality deviation in another service, is timeliness of the response. This could be measured by the number of working days from receipt to final communication with the customer on the problem.

Three days from receipt to response could be your standard or objective. Three or less would be meeting the quality objective and over three days would mean a quality deviation or lack of quality. If repeated this poor quality could mean a loss of business. In addition, failure to meet this objective continually could mean that there are inefficiencies in the investigation process or an excess volume of inquiries. Before this problem can be solved it must be identified and quality measures and standards provide the identification process. Once solved the quality objective can be met, and if the problem was an inefficiency, a cost saving would be realized. If it was due to an excess volume the characteristic which was failing and causing the high volume could be corrected and the process put back on target.

These are just a few examples of those quality measures that can be developed by identifying the key service characteristics which the customer values in each service. Setting an objective or standard of quality performance can be based upon common sense or statistics but the important aspect is *planning;* being *aware* of the level of quality today and determining where you want to be tomorrow, then *monitoring* and *controlling* in relation to that plan.

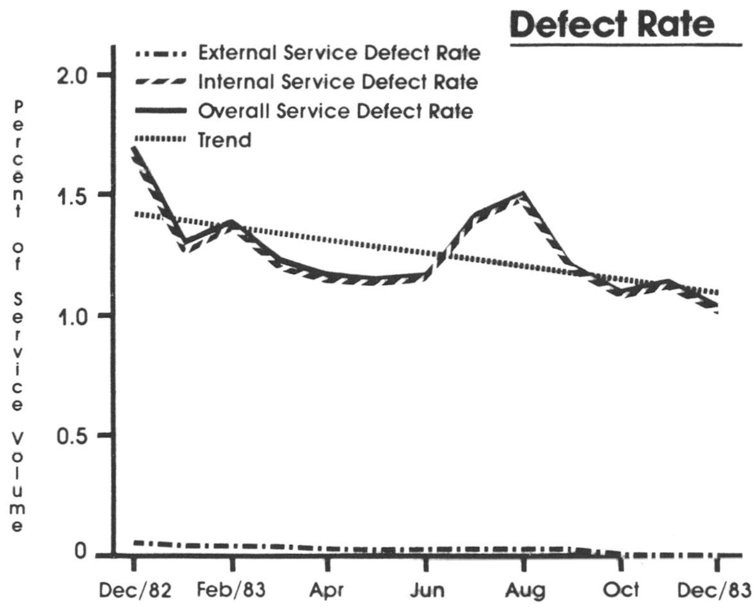
Defect Rate
External Service Defect Rate
Internal Service Defect Rate
Overall Service Defect Rate
Trend
Percent of Service Volume
2.0
1.5
1.0
0.5
0
Dec/82
Feb/83
Apr
Jun
Aug
Oct
Dec/83

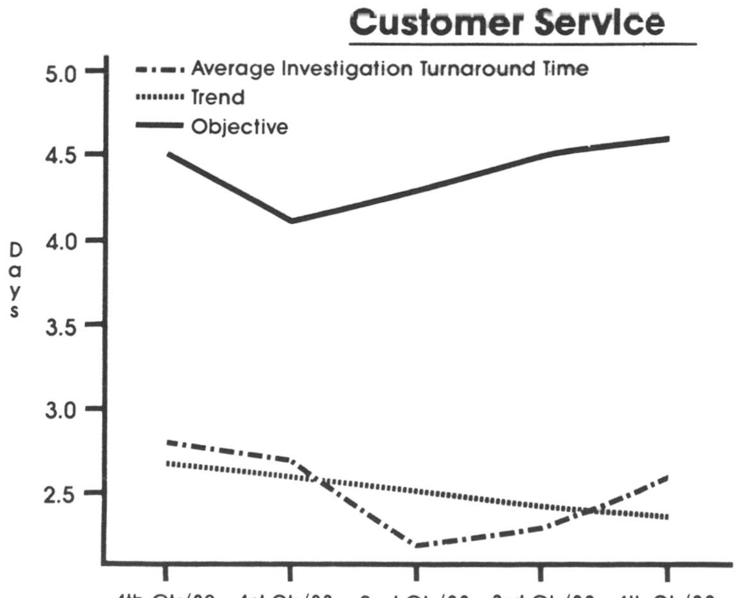
Customer Service
Average Investigation Turnaround Time
Trend
Objective
Days
5.0
4.5
4.0
3.5
3.0
2.5
4th Qtr/82
1st Qtr/83
2nd Qtr/83
3rd Qtr/83
4th Qtr/83

General examples of quality measures

OPERATIONS

Accuracy	1. Number of errors/Number of items
	2. Number of adjustments/Number of items
	3. Number of audit adjustments/Number of items
	4. Number items out of balance/Number of items
	5. Dollar errors and adjustments/Total expense

Reliability
1. On line system downtime/Time on the system
2. On line system downtime during critical period/Time of critical period

Timeliness
1. Elapsed time from receipt to processing
2. Amount of volume held over by age
3. Amount of volume held over/Total volume
4. Dollar amount held over/Dollar total received

CREDIT

Amount of Credit
1. Dollar credit received/Dollar credit requested
2. Credit requests approved/Credit requests received
3. Credit requests denied/Credit requests received

Speed of Credit
1. Elapsed time from credit request receipt to decision
2. Elapsed time from credit decision to disbursement

Effective Calling
1. Number of visits/Number of visits expected
2. Maximum number of calls per day
3. Time spent per call
4. Business gained/Number calls made

Effective Lending
1. Number charged off loans/Number of loans outstanding
2. Amount of charged off loans/Amount of loans outstanding

Experience and Knowledge
1. Number officers turned over/Number of officers
2. Number of backup officers/Account
3. Number officers trained/Number of officers
4. Number officers with number years experience/Number of officers

SECURITIES

Performance
1. Failed Securities Deliveries
2. Fails/Deliveries
3. Failed dollars
4. Failed dollars/Delivery dollars

Speed
1. Elapsed time for settlement

22

TELLER

| Speed | 1. Number of customers in the queue |
| | 2. Amount of time in the queue |

| Timeliness | 1. Time per transaction |
| | 2. Turnaround time for no-wait or mail transactions |

| Accuracy | 1. Teller differences |
| | 2. Amount charged off/Amount handled |

CUSTOMER SERVICE

| Timeliness | 1. Elapsed time from receipt of customer inquiry or problem to answer or resolution |

General	1. Number customer inquiries or problems/Number of customers
	2. Number customer inquiries or problems/Volume of service
	3. Business lost/Number of customers

PERSONNEL

| Effectiveness | 1. Number candidates rejected/Number candidates sent on interviews |
| | 2. Number days jobs have been unfilled |

STAFF PROJECT

| Timeliness | 1. Number project hours actual/Number project hours estimated |
| Effectiveness | 1. Dissatisfied users/Projects completed |

QUALITY IMPROVEMENT PROJECT

IDENTIFY: Choose operation

ANALYZE: Utilize cause and effect

ISOLATE: Verify cause

CORRECT: Implement procedures

MONITOR: Periodically review operations

CHAPTER III

Quality Costs and Productivity

Within the financial services industry as in manufacturing industry, there are costs associated with providing and ensuring a high quality product and/or service, and these costs are designated as quality costs. In order to understand the economic impact that quality costs have on the financial position of a bank, it is crucial that quality costs be defined, isolated and evaluated. The four quality cost categories of prevention, appraisal, internal failure, and external failure as they relate to financial services are defined as follows:

1. **Prevention:** Prevention costs are those costs associated with proactive measures or activities that keep failure from happening, and keep appraisal costs to a minimum. Examples of prevention activities are new product or service reviews, quality planning, quality circle meetings, training programs, written procedures, analysis of quality information and quality improvement projects.

2. **Appraisal:** Appraisal costs are those costs incurred to ascertain the condition of a product or service, in order to determine its degree of conformance to quality standards. Examples of appraisal activities are inspection of incoming work, supplies and material, periodic inspection of work in process, checking, balancing, verifying, final inspection, and collecting quality data.

3. **Internal Failure:** Internal failure costs are those costs that are incurred as a result of correcting service or products produced, not conforming to standard prior to delivery to the customer. Examples of internal failure are machine downtime, scrap due to improperly processed forms or reports, and rework or reprocessing of incorrectly processed work or transactions.

4. **External Failure:** External failure costs are those costs that are incurred as a result of correcting service or products produced, not conforming to standard after delivery to the customer or, correcting a product or service that the customer perceives does not conform to his specified standard. Examples of external failure costs are investigation time, payment of interest penalties, reprocessing of an item or transaction, scrap due to improperly processed or incorrect forms or reports, or lost or never acquired business due to providing poor service or having a poor quality reputation.

Failure costs should always be considered as the costs which would disappear if the product was defect free during or at the time of completion.

QUALITY COSTS

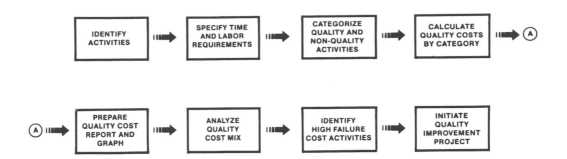

QUALITY COST WORKSHEET

OPERATION	PRE-VENTION	APPRAISAL	INTERNAL FAILURE	EXTERNAL FAILURE	NON-QUALITY
Sort Mail					X
Update Procedures	X				
Validating Future Dues		X			
Investigating Computer Rejections			X		
Mail Investigation				X	

NON-LABOR QUALITY COSTS

- **PREVENTION:**   Extra equipment on hand
- **APPRAISAL:**   Maintaining testing equipment
- **INTERNAL FAILURE:** Destroying forms
- **EXTERNAL FAILURE:** Paying interest penalties

The quality cost categories do not exist independently; in order to understand their significance to a company's quality, a basic understanding of their interrelationships is necessary. The objective in allocating resources to quality activities is that dollars spent on prevention and appraisal activities should prevent or reduce failure costs at a rate greater than 1 to 1 or for every dollar spent on prevention or appraisal more than a dollar will be saved in failure. The optimal mix of resource allocation for quality activities is the point at which an additional dollar spent on prevention or appraisal will *not* reduce failure costs at a rate greater than the additional dollar. If you continue to allocate resources to prevention and appraisal activities past the optimal point, although failure and defects will continue to be reduced, the overall effect is that *total* quality costs will increase. Customers will sometimes demand this higher level even though costs and corresponding prices are higher.

The total cost of quality cost curve can be analyzed further to determine the company's quality level based on its location on the total cost of quality curve. The curve is divided into three sections: the downward slope of the left side of the curve indicates the zone of improvement, the mid section reflects the zone of indifference, and the upward slope of the right side indicates the zone of perfection. A company's location in one of the zones is determined by its levels of quality costs. According to the model, if a company's failure costs are more than 80% and/or its prevention and appraisal costs are less than 20%, then the company is located in the improvement zone. If failure costs are approximately 50% of all quality costs and/or prevention and appraisal is approximately 50%, then the company is in the zone of indifference. If failure costs are less than 40% of quality costs and/or prevention and appraisal costs are more than 50%, then the company is in the zone of perfection. Since these ratios can vary according to industry, the service or product, or the individual customer, what may be the zone of indifference for one may be the zone of improvement for another. This is particularly true when comparing a sample model of manufacturing firms and banks to each other.

PROGRAM'S PURPOSE

The purpose of a quality cost program is to aid a company in determining by product or product line, where it is on the total cost of quality curve. The goal of the program should be to improve the company's overall quality and productivity, and hence, profitability by reducing quality costs while maintaining and/or improving high levels of quality. A quality cost program addresses various aspects of the company's profitability by answering questions as to the total cost of quality; how much is spent for each quality cost category and which products have high quality costs.

The benefits of having these questions answered systematically through a quality cost program are multi-fold. The quantitative data supplies management with necessary information so that it can optimize its resource allocation. High failure costs alert management to problems that may have been previously overlooked. As a result, improvement projects can be undertaken which rectify the situation, improve quality, and therefore productivity. A company-wide cost-of-quality program alerts the employees as to the emphasis being placed on quality, and their responsibility to meet the company's quality objectives. The company-wide commitment to quality increases productivity, since work that is done right the first time does not need to be redone. Further, increased productivity and high profitability should give the

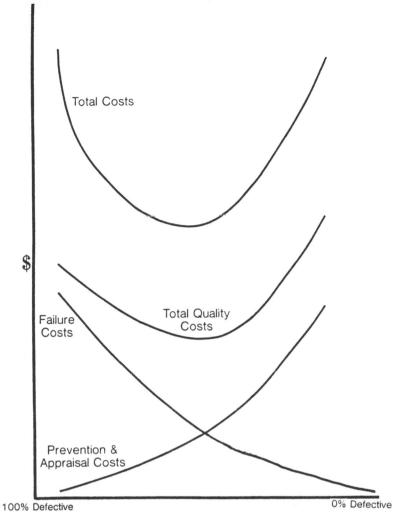

Total Costs

$

Total Quality Costs

Failure Costs

Prevention & Appraisal Costs

100% Defective

0% Defective

COMPARISON MODEL

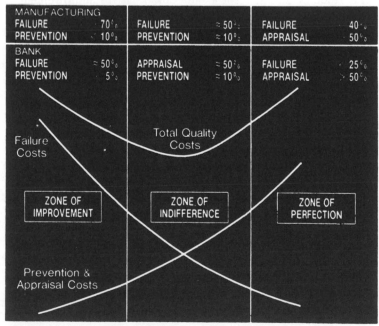

MANUFACTURING		
FAILURE 70%	FAILURE ≈ 50%	FAILURE 40%
PREVENTION 10%	PREVENTION ≈ 10%	APPRAISAL 50%
BANK		
FAILURE ≈ 50%	APPRAISAL ≈ 50%	FAILURE 25%
PREVENTION 5%	PREVENTION ≈ 10%	APPRAISAL 50%

Failure Costs

Total Quality Costs

ZONE OF IMPROVEMENT

ZONE OF INDIFFERENCE

ZONE OF PERFECTION

Prevention & Appraisal Costs

company a better position in the competitive marketplace.

These benefits, combined with emphasis on highly competitive markets with expanding product lines, and commitment to providing consistent and high levels of quality to customers, are the major forces in developing a cost of quality program.

PROGRAM IMPLEMENTATION

The success of any quality cost program is dependent on first clarifying the program's objective. The company's specific objective will determine how the program is to be implemented. However, there are basic guidelines that should be followed when implementing a quality cost program. Start small; that is to say do not attempt to quality cost every product or area within the company. Choose to examine an operation that you suspect may have high failure costs. Once you have specified the operation to be audited, collect any available financial data relating to the operation.

The company's accounting department may have some data, but their definition of cost may differ from the quality cost categories and therefore, caution should be exercised in using financial data. In addition to determining the cost of product failure in terms of scrap, warranty charges, production delays and overtime, quality costs can also be determined by breaking the operation into functions, and categorizing the time spent performing quality operations within those functions. In completing the initial study be wary of reducing the impact by spending too much time gathering the data in an attempt to be absolutely precise. The success of the initial study, and hopefully the company's cost of quality program, is that the numbers be accurate and timely when making the initial presentation to management.

The initial findings and the subsequent proposal for improvement and savings should be presented to management in terms they can understand; that of money. Explain what quality costs in dollars, as a percent of sales or unit price, as a percent of profit, or as a percent of operating expense or unit cost. Once management is aware of the significance of quality costs and its affect on the company's profitability, management should be eager to support the program downward throughout the organization. It should be stressed that without management's support, the program will not have the support or resources needed to make it successful.

When implementing a cost-of-quality program, begin by examining a division whose quality depends on offering a service which is both timely and accurate. Failure to do so costs the bank interest penalties and possibly lost business. By categorizing the functions of the service into quality and nonquality (i.e., straight production and administrative) activities, and applying direct labor expense and overhead costs to the activities, develop a cost of quality scoreboard. Present findings and the proposed cost saving project to management to gain their support. When they become aware of the significance of quality and its costs, major emphasis will be placed and resources allocated throughout the bank to monitor and improve quality through a comprehensive quality cost program. By starting small, carefully choosing a division for the initial project, and presenting findings to management, you begin the process of developing a systematic approach to implementing an organization-wide quality program.

The philosophy and initial procedure followed when starting a program is the same for a financial institution as for a manufacturing concern. However, the model that is used to develop the quality cost scoreboard differs slightly. It is significant to note that the nature of quality costs are different for a financial institution than for a manufacturing concern. A financial institution's major product is service, and therefore, labor costs comprise a major portion of all quality costs. In a manufacturing environment, product quality costs are more non-labor than labor. Consequently, the model used in developing the financial institution's quality cost scoreboard emphasizes the labor component of quality costs.

DEVELOPING A QUALITY COST SCOREBOARD

Here are two methods used in developing a quality cost scoreboard for a particular area. The first method is based on a standardized industrial engineering and costing method. The second method estimates costs based upon actual operating activity and expense, and is used when the first method is not available or feasible. Both methods require that the area's activities be specified and categorized according to quality and non-quality activities.

The standardized industrial engineering method is based on a list which enumerates operations and/or tasks performed by an area, and the standard time spent by an area to complete each operation. The quality control analyst, in conjunction with the area's management, categorize each operation as a quality or non-quality activity, and then further define the quality activities according to their appropriate quality cost category. In addition, area management completes a worksheet that lists prevention activities and the amount of time spent on each activity. The need for a prevention worksheet is that quite often, quality prevention activities are not listed on standard cost lists, and therefore, prevention costs are understated. After all quality activities have been identified, the categorized list is sent to the controllers, cost or accounting unit which determines the direct labor costs, as well as the fully absorbed cost of each quality activity based on the standard time adjusted by actual performance. The completed and adjusted categorized cost report provides the data for the quality control scoreboard.

When the standardized industrial engineering method is not practical, an operations list is developed in order to estimate costs based upon actual operating activity and expense. The list details each task or operation performed in the area and the time spent performing each task. Prevention activities and time spent performing them are also included on this list since they are part of an area's quality costs. Time can be allocated as a percentage of total available labor time or directly as total hours spent. Total hours spent performing the tasks should equal total labor hours available in the area. In either case, the total number of labor hours available in an area must be ascertained and specified. The average or actual salary level of the employee performing the task is assigned to each job. Each job is then categorized as a quality or non-quality (production) activity. Once quality activities, salary levels, and time spent performing the activities have been specified, quality costs can be calculated.

Determining quality costs is done in two steps. First determine the labor cost of each quality activity, and then the overhead cost, in order to derive the fully absorbed cost of each quality activity. Direct labor cost is calculated by a two step process.

First, the salary level or hourly wage that is associated with each quality activity, is multiplied by the hours associated with that activity. ($5.60/hour $\times$ 6.5 hours). Additional costs (i.e., fringe benefits) associated with labor costs are directly added or factored into the salary or hourly wages. ($32.5 + 6.5 $\times$ $1.50 or $32.5 $\times$ 1.3). The resulting product is the labor cost of performing each quality activity.

The expense statement is analyzed to determine if any other direct expenses are quality cost items; if so, they are assigned to a specific quality cost category. Examples of other direct expenses are: having extra equipment on hand for possible machine downtime (an example of prevention) purchasing/maintaining MICR testing equipment (an example of appraisal) destroying forms (an example of internal failure) and paying interest penalties (an example of external failure).

Overhead cost for quality activities can be calculated in one of two ways. The monthly expense statement specifies the amount of non-labor expense which is then divided by the total number of full time people working within the area. This number is then divided by 172 in order to determine the hourly overhead expense rate. The overhead hourly expense rate is then multiplied by the hours spent performing each quality activity, in order to derive the overhead cost of performing each quality activity.

The second method of calculating overhead cost is done in the aggregate. The difference between the total expense and the total salary expense represents the overhead expense for the period. The overhead expense is then divided by the total salary expense to determine the ratio of a salary dollar to an overhead dollar. This percentage is then multiplied to the labor cost associated with performing each quality activity to determine the overhead cost of performing each activity.

The labor cost and the overhead cost of each quality activity are then summed to determine the fully absorbed or total cost of each quality activity. The fully absorbed costs of each quality activity within a particular cost category are totalled to determine the individual cost category's contribution to the total cost of quality. The individual categories' totals can be compared to each other, as well as to the area's total expenses, to provide additional feedback as to the significance of quality costs.

BENEFITS OF A QUALITY COST SCOREBOARD

The cost-of-quality scoreboard provides valuable information that can be used to evaluate quality levels in the aggregate, and individually. In the aggregate, the quality cost scoreboard highlights trends in the company's quality expenditures, and the results of the expenditures as they affect quality. Decisions can be made in part by analyzing the interrelationships between the various quality cost categories. A profitable product line or service with low failure costs could be expanded, while a low profit product line or service with high failure costs could be justifiably discontinued if failure costs could not be reduced. High failure costs could alert the manager to various existing problems or negative trends. High prevention and/or appraisal costs for a relatively insignificant product, could signal an inefficient resource allocation. Operations with small amounts of prevention and appraisal, but with high failure costs, could increase their prevention and appraisal activities in order to reduce failure costs and improve quality. By measuring the amount of prevention and appraisal, as compared to the amount of internal and external failure, a manager can determine if his resource allocation is being optimized.

Although evaluating the quality cost scoreboard in the aggregate provides valuable feedback for monitoring quality, the scoreboard is particularly beneficial in highlighting problem operations. Quality cost data can identify a problem operation that could be improved by implementing a quality improvement project in order to reduce quality costs while improving quality.

The success of a quality improvement project depends on accurately applying cause and effect analysis to the problem. The quality cost data indicates the symptom or effect, but until the causes are known, identified, and tested, no action should be taken to correct the problem. To attempt to solve a problem without knowing the cause would only increase quality costs and negate the purpose of the quality cost program. Having properly identified the cause or causes of the problem, the manager can use the improvement project to set goals and a course of action to correct the problem. He can then estimate potential savings based on the proposed course of action. The manager can begin to evaluate the success of the improvement project and the quality cost program, by measuring the actual progress in reducing quality costs, while maintaining or improving quality compared to the goals of the program that were initially established.

In objectively evaluating the success of quality improvement projects or a quality cost program, caution must be taken when measuring success by comparing performance to standard. Very often, the standard is based on historical data which has high levels of failure built into it; therefore to measure progress of recent actions to it may be painting a prettier picture of success than actually exists. Although comparison to the historical standard is a place to begin, a more meaningful measure of success is to periodically evaluate quality costs and compare the periodic totals to

QUALITY COST REPORT

SECTION/OPERATION	PRE-VENTION	APPRAISAL	INTERNAL FAILURE	EXTERNAL FAILURE	TOTAL
Validating Future Dues	0	350	0	0	350
Mail Investigation	0	0	0	6,600	6,600
Total Cost of Quality	15,200	48,700	4,100	39,000	107,100
Cost of Quality as a % of Total Quality Costs	14%	46%	4%	36%	100%
Cost of Quality as a % of Total Expense	4%	13%	1%	11%	29%

each other. Objectively evaluating the success of quality improvement projects and the quality cost program also depends on the accuracy of the data. It is crucial to collect and report cost data consistently and accurately when attempting to accurately evaluate the reduction of quality costs, and therefore, the success of the program. Inconsistent and inaccurate reporting skews the results of the quality cost scoreboard, and therefore, discounts the validity of the quality cost program.

Finally, by using the quality cost scoreboard to evaluate trends, isolate problem areas, and measure overall quality improvement based on cost reductions, the manager can reevaluate his operating budget, and therefore, allocate his resources more effectively.

FINANCIAL SERVICES EXPERIENCE

Use your quality cost scoreboard to more accurately measure the quality of the services you provide, and the cost of providing such service. Evaluating your location on the total cost-of-quality curve is not as quantifiable as in manufacturing. Generally, a company determines its position on the total cost curve, or stated otherwise, its optimal quality cost mixture, by comparing its performance to similar companies, or by establishing acceptable ratios of quality costs categories as compared to each other, or as compared to another meaningful measure, e.g., profits or sales. However, the nature of our business (the user of funds as a significant resource) has traditionally precluded financial institutions from effectively measuring their quality costs compared to sales or profits. Nor have financial institutions published or even established quality cost scoreboards. When analyzed, developed, and compared to other institutions perceived quality and quality costs they would offer an indication of their proper location on the quality cost curve. Therefore, you can analyze your success in achieving your quality cost program objectives of improving quality and productivity, while reducing quality costs, without increasing other costs. This can be done by evaluating the interrelationships of the quality cost categories, and by implementing quality improvement projects.

In evaluating the interrelationships between the quality cost categories and their relationship to total expenses, we find that the financial services quality cost mix model differs from the manufacturing mix. Although one must be careful to generalize from company to company or from industry to industry, experience has shown that for a manufacturing company, prevention costs are usually .5 to 5% of all quality costs, appraisal is 10 to 50%, internal failure is 24-50%, and external failure is 20-40% of total quality costs. A bank's quality cost scoreboard does not reflect these ratios. The major reason for this difference can be found in the difference of financial products versus the products offered by a manufacturing concern. A manufacturing company sells a product that is tangible, and therefore much more quantifiable than the financial services. Hence, measuring the quality of a manufacturer's product as it conforms to specified standards, is easier than measuring if a financial service satisfies the customer's expectations, which is dictated by the customers individual desires or needs. Therefore, inherent in our business of processing financial transactions accurately and on-time, is the need for extensive "upfront" and "through put" quality controls. As a result of this need, financial services' appraisal costs as

QUALITY COSTS IN MANAGERIAL TERMS

- Quality costs as a percent of net interest and operating income —
  $31.4M/$1,008.2M = 3.12%

- Quality costs as a potential contributor to net income —
  Failure cost savings increase net income by $5.6M or 2.2%

- Quality costs as a potential contributor to earnings per share —
  Failure cost savings increase EPS by 14.1¢ share = $5.6M/39.6M shares

- Quality costs in dollars — **$31.4M**

- Quality costs as a portion of unit price —
  $5/wire transfer = $1.70 quality cost or 34%

- Quality costs as portion of unit cost —
  $4.50/wire transfer = $1.70 quality cost or 38%

- Quality costs as a percent of operating expense —
  $31.4M/$623.9M = 5%

QUALITY COST IMPROVEMENT

QUALITY OPERATION	MAR/ 81	JUNE/ 81	SEPT/ 81	DEC/ 81	MAR/ 82
Telex Investigations	4,325	4,200	3,600	3,200	3,200

a percent of total quality costs tend to be much greater than the corresponding appraisal percentages experienced in manufacturing. Not surprisingly, failure costs tend to be significantly lower than those in manufacturing.

Financial institutions which have quality cost scoreboards have yielded interesting and consistent results. When quality costs represent more than 50% of total expense, internal and external failure costs are less than 50% of prevention and appraisal costs. This would seem to indicate that organizations that have proportionately high quality costs are aware of the need to appraise their service prior to delivering the service, and by doing so, failure costs are kept to a minimum. Those organizations whose quality costs are proportionately small compared to overall expense, spend approximately equal amounts on prevention and appraisal, as compared to internal and external failure, and their failure costs are substantially higher. This would suggest that these organizations are prime candidates for a quality improvement project.

Although evaluating the interrelationships between the cost categories and resulting trends provides valuable feedback, a quality cost scoreboard does not automatically place you at a certain point on the total cost of quality curve, based on the manufacturing quality cost mix model. Whereas appraisal costs that are greater than 50% of all quality costs may signify the perfection zone for a manufacturing concern, 50% appraisal for a financial institution may represent the zone of indifference. Again, this is directly attributable to the nature of the financial services industry which inherently emphasizes and practices prevention and appraisal activities. Further, failure costs that represent 50% of all quality costs may place a manufacturing concern in the zone of indifference, whereas failure costs representing 50% of total quality costs may place a bank in the improvement zone. Although the total cost of quality curve is the same for manufacturing and financial services, it would appear that the mixes that comprise the zones of improvement, indifference, and perfection vary.

If this is true, then how can you use the quality cost scoreboard to determine your location on the curve and your course of action? We are assuming that for all products you have not yet attained the optimal quality cost mix, where an increase in prevention and appraisal costs does not reduce internal and external failure costs at a greater rate than the increase. Although in the aggregate you may be in the zone of perfection, you want to carefully examine the location on the total quality cost curve of each individual unit and product line that comprises the aggregate.

Next complete quality improvement projects for each unit for which a cost of quality audit has been completed. The projects are aimed at reducing the failure costs of the activity in the unit which has the highest failure costs. If failure costs can and are reduced, without increasing total quality costs, while maintaining or improving quality, then you have succeeded in accomplishing the program's goal. If increasing prevention and appraisal costs does not reduce failure costs more than proportionally, then the optimal quality cost mix has been attained.

QUALITY COST PROCESS

The purpose of developing quality costs is threefold. The first objective of quality costs is to make management aware of the magnitude of quality costs and encourage proper managerial attention to quality and quality functions. The second objective is to help an area determine its current quality cost mix and whether or not adjustments should be made. The third objective of the quality cost study is to highlight any activities that have high failure costs associated with them. Activities with high failure costs can be identified as potential candidates for quality improvement projects. The successful completion of quality improvement projects can lead to substantial reduction in failure and rework costs, which ultimately results in higher productivity. Quality costs development can be broken into three parts: 1) data collection; 2) report preparation; and 3) analysis and feedback. To develop quality costs in a particular area, each activity done within the area is listed. Once the activities are listed, the supervisor enumerates how many people perform the activity, the salary level of each individual, and how much time is spent performing each activity. If time spent is not readily available, samples can be taken or work measurement can be used. Time can be specified as a percentage of a working day/week/month or in absolute hours.

The labor time shown on the report should balance to the total amount of labor time available in the area, including the supervisor's time. All the activities should be categorized into quality or non-quality activities. Non-quality activities are those activities which are considered strictly production or administration oriented. The identified quality activities are then categorized by specific quality cost category. It should be stressed that an activity can be part production/administration and part quality. An activity can be comprised of two or more quality components.

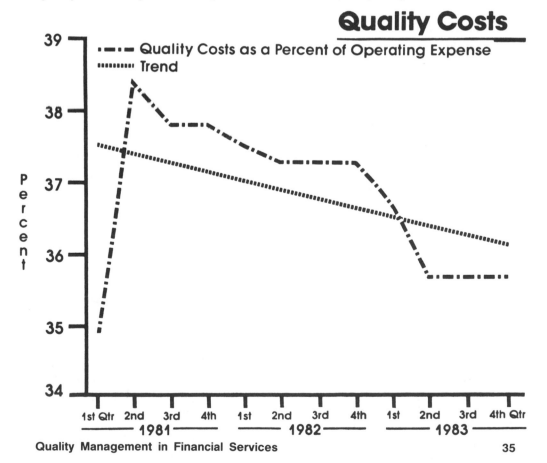

Quality Costs

· —· — Quality Costs as a Percent of Operating Expense
·········· Trend

In preparing the report, each quality activity is first sorted according to type, (prevention, appraisal, internal, and external failure), and is then costed out to determine each activity's cost, as well as each quality cost category's total. To determine the quality cost of a particular quality activity, the number of hours per month spent performing the activity is calculated. The appropriate labor cost per hour is determined by multiplying the midpoint of the salary level by a factor of 1.xx which allows for fringe benefits associated with a basic salary. A particular activity's cost is the product of multiplying the adjusted salary rate by the total labor hours spent. If more than one employee salary level performs an activity, the weighted average of the adjusted salary levels of all individuals performing that function are calculated when determining the cost of the activity.

An area's non-labor costs should also be reviewed and analyzed for their quality cost contribution. Examples of quality-related, non-labor costs are: having extra equipment on hand for possible machine downtime (an example of prevention), purchasing/maintaining MICR testing equipment (an example of appraisal), destroying forms which were prepared incorrectly (an example of internal failure), and paying interest penalties (an example of external failure).

The calculations are completed when the quality costs of all activities are totaled by category to determine the total and the percentage each quality cost category contributes to overall quality costs. Each category's total is also contrasted to the area's overall expense figure to provide further comparison of quality costs to overall area expense.

After the calculations are complete, the findings are analyzed and a summary with recommendations is prepared. The analysis highlights the magnitude of the quality costs, the area's quality cost mix and specific high failure costs. The analysis will suggest a future course of action. One potential course of action is quality improvement projects.

Generally, this is indicated when the optimum quality cost mix has not been attained. Specific quality improvement projects are indicated when a particular activity has high failure costs associated with it. The objectives in undertaking a quality improvement project are to reduce quality and total costs (or at least change the quality cost mix) while improving actual quality levels.

Quality improvement projects are not necessarily complex or difficult, and can yield a high payback without expending large amounts of money and/or time.

CASE STUDY

A quality cost study was done in a loan processing section after developing quality costs for the area. The study showed that the activity "processing holdouts," which is defined as computer tickets that are rejected during daily processing, represented failure costs of more than $2,000 per month. Holdouts accounted for 30% of all tickets processed. In order to reprocess the holdouts, the reason for the reject had to be determined, and the tickets were held for next day processing. The delay prevented updating lending information accurately and timely. This information is needed to determine a customer's credit availability, the bank's credit exposure and the bank's financial statements.

Prior to developing quality costs, the loan processing area had not been aware of the magnitude of quality costs, and in particular, the holdout problem as evidenced by its high monthly failure cost. The area was enthusiastic about initiating a quality improvement project in an effort to reduce holdouts, lower costs and increase quality. Since the cause of the excessive number of holdouts was unknown, the quality improvement project began with data collection.

In an effort to identify the problem, the area supervisor kept a holdout log. Each holdout was listed by the type of error that caused the reject, as well as the clerk who submitted it. Pareto analysis was done to determine which errors occurred most frequently and which clerks were responsible for the greatest number of errors. A matrix was constructed to see if there was a correlation between the two.

After completing the Pareto analysis, it was found that three types of errors were primarily responsible for the rejected tickets and that three clerks were responsible for the majority of the errors. The actual production operation was carefully monitored to determine the cause of the high error rates by certain clerks and the types of errors. Particular attention was paid to the quality of the incoming information and to how the clerk transferred it onto the computer input tickets. Further, the rejected tickets that were resubmitted were monitored to determine if they were again rejected. Since it was the responsibility of the clerk to determine the cause of the initial rejection and correct it, a twice rejected ticket might indicate that the clerk was unsure as to how to correct the error. It was found that few tickets were rejected twice which indicated that the clerks knew how to correct a rejected ticket.

Observations identified possible causes of the high error rates which were responsible for the rejected tickets. Frequently, incomplete or unclear information was received and some of the clerks were unsure as to how to proceed with the processing. Knowing the need for immediacy in processing, the clerks attempted to process the less than perfect information. It appeared that there was not a consistent method of completing input tickets since each clerk had his/her own method of completion. Further, since the supervisor had not been closely monitoring the holdouts, she was not giving the clerks necessary feedback or suggesting corrective action for the most frequently occurring errors.

These observations suggested multiple courses of action which were acted upon. Each clerk was required to participate in a training program in order to insure a uniform understanding of section and ticket processing procedures. A comprehensive procedures manual was written to accompany the training program and to serve as ready reference for the clerks. Clerks were encouraged to ask the senior clerk or supervisor questions concerning processing of non-routine items. By asking for clarification upfront, prevention and appraisal activities were being performed in order to reduce failure costs later. Additional appraisal activities were now being performed by the clerks. They were instructed to reject input information that was incomplete or unclear and return it to the initiator, instead of attempting to process it and hoping it "would pass." By returning bad input to the user, the loan area was giving the user important feedback regarding their quality. This improved the quality of the input to the loan area.

The analysis had shown that the errors which occurred most frequently were caused by not matching two critical fields on the input ticket. As a result, the training course stressed that the clerks pay particular attention to correctly completing the matching fields.

The supervisor was encouraged to take greater initiative in measuring (sampling) the frequency and types of errors that were occurring as well as giving clerks frequent feedback. By monitoring the types of errors, the frequency and the person responsible, the supervisor could resolve or correct a potential problem before quality would be severely affected. The frequent feedback made the clerks more aware and more responsible for the quality of their work. Together, the supervisor and clerks worked to attack poor quality symptoms before they became quality problems.

Six months after initially developing quality costs, the costs were reviewed. The suggestions resulted in a shift of the area's quality cost mix, and a reduction in overall quality costs and total costs, as well as improved quality. The training and feedback increased the prevention and appraisal activities of both the supervisor and the clerks. Failure costs decreased by over $1,000 per month while quality improved 25%, since rejects were virtually eliminated. The time the supervisor spent writing the procedures manual and developing the training were considered one-time costs; while the ongoing training and review of the clerks was considered part of the supervisor's basic responsibilities.

IMPACT ON PRODUCTIVITY

The overall effects of quality costs and their improvement also can be observed by productivity measurement.

Productivity is measured by an output/input equation which yields an index. Tracking this index over time indicates the productivity trend. The numerator specifies the volume of the item processed during the month. The denominator includes the volume of resources expended to process the numerator volume.

Therefore, productivity can be positively affected by a change in the quality cost mix if failure costs are reduced.

A productivity measure was developed for the same area for which we just measured quality costs. The numerator specifies the number of tickets processed during the month. The denominator lists the resources incurred to process the tickets, which included: labor hours, computer run time and ticket forms. Thus the measure appears as follows:

$$\frac{\text{Tickets Processed}}{\text{Labor} + \text{Systems} + \text{Forms}}$$

Since labor hours, systems and forms cannot be added together, a base period cost was assigned to each resource. The base costs do not change over time, only the amount of resources used. The base period cost of labor was $11.13 per hour, systems processing was a fixed $500 rate for the month, and forms were $.05 apiece.

At the time that quality costs were initially developed, approximately 2,080 tickets were processed per month at a cost of $7,753. Labor represented $7,123 ($11.13 × 640 hours), systems $500 and forms $130 ($.05 × 2600 forms). The productivity index was calculated to be 26.83.

$$\frac{2,080}{(\$11.13 \times 640) + \$500 + (\$.05 \times 2600)} = \frac{2,080}{\$7,123 + \$500 + \$130} = 26.83$$

After the quality improvement project was completed, the productivity index was recalculated. Productivity had improved as evidenced by the increased index. Slightly more tickets were processed with less resources expended.

The new productivity measure appears as follows:

$$\frac{2,100}{(\$11.13 \times 546) + \$500 + (\$.05 \times 2100)} = \frac{2,100}{\$6,077 + \$500 + \$105} = 31.43$$

The new index represented an increase from the earlier productivity index, and a 17% increase in productivity.

This index confirmed that the process productivity had improved. Approximately the same number of tickets were processed, but the amount of labor and forms used decreased, since holdouts were eliminated.

Other divisions in the bank noticed the improvement of quality within the loan processing section because of the timeliness and accuracy with which the area posted critical information.

The importance of a comprehensive quality program cannot be overstated. When an operation's quality performance is poor, a quality standards program can alert an area to a potential quality problem. Some potential quality problems can be verified by developing quality costs. Quality costs can also alert an area to quality problems that may not be evident by traditional quality standards, as was seen in the case study. The inordinate amount of rejects was not apparent from measuring performance to standard or productivity. Only after developing quality costs was the problem identified and resolved. Once activities with high failure costs are identified, action can be taken to correct the specific problem. This will reduce failure activities and their failure costs, improve quality, and therefore, productivity.

Productivity

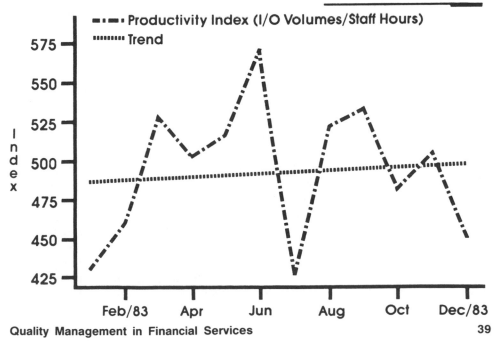

CHAPTER IV

Quality Control Circles

Quality Circles are small groups of people who do similar work, and voluntarily meet on a regular basis to identify and analyze causes of problems, recommend their solutions to management, and where possible, implement the solutions themselves. It is important to initially understand that a Quality Circle is not a "program" with a designated end, nor a cure-all for every quality or employee-relations problem. Quality Circles are a process, not a program, but an on-going process, one that can supplement current managerial practices and benefit the whole organization. It is a commitment to a particular management style intended to maximize people resources through capturing and utilizing the creative and innovative power within the workforce. With proper presentation, education, and conformance to basic principles, Quality Circles can be an integral part of the quality management process by insuring high quality services and contributing to greater satisfaction among the workforce.

HISTORY

Quality Circles originated in Japan in the early 1960's in response to a critical economic need to overcome its reputation as the source of cheap, poorly made goods. Merging behavioral theories with the quality control sciences introduced in Japan by Drs. Deming and Juran created a "system" called Quality Control Circles. In 1961, a series of exploratory meetings were sponsored by the Union of Japanese Scientists and Engineers (JUSE) under the leadership of Dr. Kaoru Ishikawa, an engineering professor at the University of Tokyo. The objective was to develop a way to allow the hands-on workers the opportunity to contribute to the benefit of the company. In 1962, the first Circle was registered with JUSE, and a total of 20 were registered and operating by the end of the year. Since that time, the Quality Circle techniques have been taught to and applied by the total Japanese workforce. Today, there are an estimated one million Quality Circles in Japan with over ten million members. In addition, these Quality Circles have been considered a major contributor to Japan's present status as a leader in both quality and productivity.

Quality Circles

Small groups of people who are <u>trained in problem-solving techniques</u> and <u>voluntarily</u> meet on a <u>regular</u> basis to <u>develop improvements</u>, or to solve their <u>common work-related problems</u>; finding causes, <u>implementing solutions</u> or <u>proposing recommendations</u> to management when necessary.

Quality Circles were first introduced in the United States in 1970 by a large manufacturing company (Lockheed Aircraft). The success of the Lockheed program, combined with the company's enthusiasm in publicizing and promoting their implementation process and results, has encouraged other American companies to adopt this management style. Initially, Circles were almost exclusively limited to manufacturing industries, but recently, they have been successfully introduced into service industries as well. Currently, in the United States, there are in excess of 5,000 Circles and 50,000 members in over 400 companies. It is for good reason that the Quality Circle concept has been called, "One of the most fascinating movements of the past few explosive years in management/employee and organizational development."

QUALITY CIRCLE PROCESS

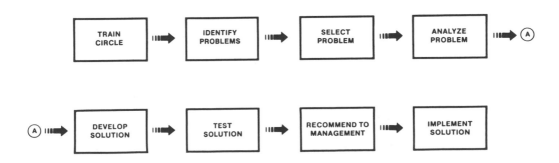

PHILOSOPHY

The underlying Quality Circle philosophy is based on the belief that employees will take more pride and interest in their work if they are allowed to make meaningful contributions which influence decisions made about their work.

Active employee participation and involvement in the decision-making process increases feelings of satisfaction, pride, accomplishment, and interest in work; employees are able to express their work-related concerns, improve their jobs, and contribute to the fulfillment of organizational goals and objectives. A crucial premise is that the individual who is doing the job is the expert and knows best how the work should be done. By giving the employees input into decisions regarding their work, management acknowledges that the workers are a vast reservoir of knowledge and ideas. Quality Circles are meant to bring human abilities into full play and reveal the unlimited potential of the workforce. In this sense, Circle implementation symbolizes the company's endorsement of the creativity and "brainpower" waiting to be expressed within the workforce.

The Quality Circle philosophy evolved through a merging of behavioral and quality control sciences. McGregor, Herzberg, and Maslow are three key social scientists whose ideas formed the basis of present Quality Circle beliefs.

McGregor's "Theory Y" is the underlying attitude adopted in Quality Circle application. McGregor attached the "Y" label to managerial behavior which recognizes the intellectual and creative potential of the average human being. Quality Circles utilize this potential by involving people at all employment levels in solving quality or other work-related problems. By giving employees training, time, and recognition, the corporation is stating that it believes employees have meaningful contributions to make.

Frederick Herzberg's motivation theory is another management philosophy serving as a foundation for the Quality Circle approach. In developing and promoting this theory, Herzberg stresses that maturation is derived from the content of the job itself. Factors which contribute to the fulfillment of a job are the opportunity for new learning, direct communication between management and employees, constant feedback, and personal accountability. Quality Circles provide expression of these factors especially in repetitious, boring, or monotonous job situations.

The hierarchy of needs which Maslow identified as being inherent in all human beings, has been a tool used by managers to understand what motivates their employees. When employees channel their energies at work to achieve "self-actualization," increased interest in and motivation towards their work is apparent. Quality Circles provide workers with a vehicle for attaining personal goals and fulfilling their motivation needs.

Transforming these behavioral science concepts into operational guidelines enables the Circle philosophy to be both theoretically sound and functionally applicable.

Behavioral Science Concept	Quality Circle Application
• Management must be committed to a change effort and all involved in its initiation.	• A Quality Circle effort is initiated only upon the decision of senior management.
	• Participation in the Circle is voluntary.
• People should have control in deciding or changing work elements close to them.	• Circles are made up of workers with a common area of interest and intervention. Changes have to do with the work that each person does daily. Only the most advanced Circles work on interdepartmental issues.
• Individuals should not be coerced to change.	• Participation in a Circle is voluntary. Participants work on problems they decide need to be worked on in their own priority order.
• Work should be intrinsically motivating and enriching.	• New skills regarding problem solving, statistics and measurement are taught to Circle members which enrich their lives and are seen as interesting.
• Any change effort should be monitored and measured for impact.	• All Quality Circle activities are monitored and measured constantly. The major efforts of a Circle involve measuring current performance, initiating or constructing change and measuring results.
• Jobs need feedback to be reinforcing.	• A QC Circle is a feedback device. It is built on the basis of feedback and measurement.
• Workers need opportunities to meet higher motivational needs through the job.	• The intrinsic value of seeing change and improvement, coupled with the regular management presentation, gives visibility, exposure, and ownership of results that few other change interventions allow.
	• The time off the job for the Circle to meet provides its own brand of recognition. So does the social need that members address with each other.

PRACTICE

Actual Quality Circle practice closely relates to the underlying Circle philosophy. In order for the Quality Circle experience to be successful, these elements must be maintained and followed.

The Quality Circles implemented must have as their *primary objective the development of the Circle Members' individual capabilities—people-building.* If Circles are used by management solely as a cost reduction program, or to manipulate employees for the organization's benefit, the program will fail.

Management of all levels must openly and unreservedly support Circle efforts. Managers and supervisors should not feel threatened, or take credit away from the Circle when improvements are made. If managers do not become involved in Quality Circle activities, they may feel by-passed or lacking in authority. Involvement in the activities will enhance contact and trust between managers and Circle members, and therefore, promote better communications.

Membership in Quality Circles must be voluntary. If employees are forced to participate, they will feel that the program is just a facade, or a management gimmick to make people work harder.

Team spirit and group effort should be incited. Projects are not individual efforts. Circle Members should solve the problems together and help each other develop and learn. No criticism of people is allowed. The focus of the group must be the problem, and not the people creating problems or contributing ideas. Circle meetings are not "gripe" sessions.

Creativity and innovation must be encouraged. Creative methods are taught to the group, and a nonthreatening, open atmosphere should be established and maintained.

The projects selected by the Circle Members are related to their work. The Steering Committee sets the goals, objectives and policies, and the Circles choose the themes and procedures to meet those goals. Members become more responsible for their work when involved in making decisions regarding it.

Practical training in problem-solving techniques must be provided and utilized. It is essential that Circle Members have the tools and skills needed to find solutions and make recommendations on the projects they select. Circle meetings cannot be viewed as a way to "get out of work" for an hour each week. The Leader must insure that no Members dominate the discussions, or, conversely, feel limited in what they can express and contribute.

In addition to the people-building aspect of Quality Circles, an equally important goal stated by Ishikawa is the emphasis on quality awareness and improvement among the workforce. Developing a problem-solving capability in the employees and an attitude of "problem prevention" are reinforced throughout Circle activities. Working on quality issues is the disciplining structure for Quality Circle involvement and interaction. Not only does this structure prevent the meetings from becoming "gripe" sessions, but many times the solutions recommended by the Circles result in substantial cost savings and productivity improvements. So in addition to increased feelings of accomplishment and satisfaction among the Circle members, active employee participation and involvement promote and enhance quality and productivity, reduce costs, and ultimately contribute to the fulfillment of personal and organization goals and objectives.

If the Quality Circle process is to be implemented and operated effectively, the organization must consider and embrace the basic principles and goals which reflect the underlying philosophy.

- *Trust your employees.* Expect that they will work to implement organization goals if given a chance.
- *Build employee loyalty to the company.* It will pay off.
- *Invest in training, and treat employees as resources which, if cultivated, will yield economic returns to the firm.* This means developing employee skills . . . aiming for long-term employee commitment to the organization.
- *Recognize employee accomplishments.* Symbolic rewards mean more than you think.
- *Decentralize decision making.* Train employees to make decisions which will eliminate bottlenecks waiting for responses.
- *Regard work as a cooperative effort, with workers and managers doing the job together.* This implies consensual decision making.

When an organization believes in these principles, or begins to move toward the management style implicit in them, it is totally prepared to begin the implementation process. Don Dewar, Quality Circle consultant, stresses that modifications of the process or program developed in Japan are made at the company's own risk. Failure is most likely to occur in companies where Quality Circles have deviated from the Japanese model.

ORGANIZATION OF THE QUALITY CIRCLE

The Circle consists of three to eleven voluntary members (ideal size 7 or 8) who have a shared area of responsibility. Historically, the work functions of the Circle Members are of a low grade level, although there have been Circles composed of managerial grade personnel. The Members meet on a regular basis to receive training in problem prevention, identification, analysis, measurement techniques, and presentation skills which help them identify, select and analyze quality problems, and propose solutions to them.

The Leader of a Circle is usually the Circle Members' work area supervisor. It is the responsibility of the Leader to train Circle Members (with the assistance of the Facilitator), to insure the smooth and effective operation of the Circle, and to involve each member as many times as possible at each meeting. In addition to problem identification, analysis, and measurement skills, the Leader also receives training in the areas of Group Dynamics, Leadership Skills, Motivation and Communication Techniques. He/she is trained to work as a Member, not as a "boss."

The Company or Corporate Facilitator of Quality Circles is on staff to a company official who is a strong supporter of Circle activities. He/she organizes and works with the Circles on a gradually decreasing basis, until the Circles are self-directing and self-perpetuating. *The Company Facilitator trains the Circle Leaders and Departmental Facilitators.* In addition, he/she assists the Leader in training the Circle Members. When technical experts must be called in to assist the Circle, it is

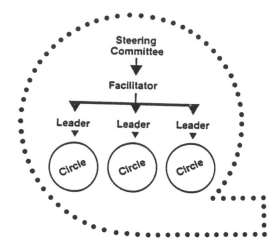

Quality Circles Organization

- Circles: 3 to 12 Members who identify, analyze and solve quality problems in their work areas

- Leaders: Supervisors who direct Circles and train Members

- Facilitator: the individual responsible for coordinating and directing Quality Circles' activities and training Leaders

- Steering Committee: 5 to 15 members who establish goals, objectives and operational guidelines for Quality Circle activities

the Facilitator who arranges this assistance, and assures that the experts act only as consultants, rather than taking control of the group's activities. Helping the Circle Leader and the Members communicate the results of their efforts to management and the organization is the responsibility of the Facilitator. He/she must coordinate the publication of the Circle's progress in outside journals, as well as in-house publications.

In large or complex organizations, it may be necessary to select Departmental Facilitators. In this case, *the Departmental Facilitator is on staff to the head of the department or divisions where Circles are implemented.* He/she reports to the Department Head for appraisal and salary, but reports to the Company Facilitator on Circle activities, progress, and assistance. The Departmental Facilitator works very closely with his/her departmental Circles on training and problem-solving. When there is a necessity for a Departmental Facilitator, it is important that his/her responsibilities are kept detailed and separate from those of the Company Facilitator to minimize overlap in their functions. Both types of Facilitators must have the capabilities for and responsibilities of being promoter, coach, teacher, coordinator, and liaison between all levels of management and employees.

The last essential element of the Quality Circles organizational structure, *the Steering Committee, is composed of managers and top staff personnel, and includes the Facilitator. The Committee's purpose is to set objectives (what is to be accomplished), goals (how these are to be accomplished), and milestones (when these should be accomplished) for the Circles.* It establishes operational guidelines and the rate of expansion. The Steering Committee chooses Departmental Facilitators as needed, and determines funding arrangements for Circle training and activities. In addition, the Steering Committee has the responsibility for publicizing, promoting

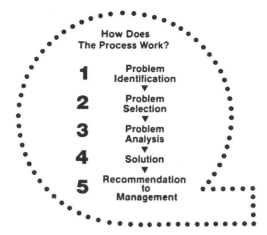

How Does The Process Work?

1 Problem Identification
   ▼
2 Problem Selection
   ▼
3 Problem Analysis
   ▼
4 Solution
   ▼
5 Recommendation to Management

Quality Circle Operation

Quality Circle Implementation and Operation Sequence

- Explore the use of Quality Circles as an effective method of improving quality and motivating employees to achieve high quality standards
- Assess the readiness of the division(s) to implement Quality Circles
- Decide to implement Circles
- Establish and familiarize the Steering Committee with the Quality Circle philosophy
- Develop an implementation plan
- Set operational parameters and Circle objectives
- Select and train Facilitators
- Select and train Leaders
- Implement Middle-Management Support Training
- Quality Circle potential Member volunteers oriented
- Quality Circles meet weekly
  - Quality Circle Members trained
  - Quality Circles Identify and Solve Problems
  - Quality Circles develop improvements
- Steering Committee meets monthly; reviews objectives and milestones
- Quality Circles make management presentations
- Quality Circle activities receive recognition

and educating people about the Quality Circles approach and progress. A chairman presides over the democratic processes of the Committee.

After this organizational structure has been established for Pilot Circles, and the Quality Circle approach has been approved by senior level management, implementation and operation begins.

IMPLEMENTATION, TRAINING AND OPERATION

S. Boon, consultant and training specialist with Quality Control Circles, Inc., outlined the Quality Circle process as basically consisting of four steps. These steps are: (1) *Opportunity,* (2) *Training,* (3) *Results,* and (4) *Recognition.* All successful Quality Circle implementations must go through each one of these steps to insure the proper initiation and expansion of the Quality Circle concept. Followed in sequence, and used properly, this Circle process can provide a more effective way to manage and motivate people.

OPPORTUNITY

Implementation starts with an explanation of the Circle concept to management and to the workers. All levels of management must be involved. The go-ahead on Circles comes from upper management, but its approval goes through a filter of many levels before it reaches the workers. The *first step in the process, after receiving approval, is to familiarize upper management and the Steering Committee with Circle philosophy and techniques.* It is crucial at this point that Steering Committee members thoroughly understand the implications of Circle activities and the role that they must play in gaining support and enthusiasm from their supervisors and workers. To facilitate this process, it is recommended that managers receive a formal orientation to the Circle concept (preferably a detailed training on Quality Circle techniques) so they have a clear understanding of the purpose and goals of the Circles. The next step is to specifically consider what actions managers should take to publicly express their support of the process and heighten awareness of the Circle concept among the workforce. Simply supporting the process is not enough— managers must provide evidence to workers that Circles will be supported on a day-to-day basis. Some examples of actions they can take are:

- Serving on a Steering Committee
- Authorizing work hours for Circle meetings
- Releasing top notch personnel to serve as Facilitators
- Authorizing funds for supplies needed by Circles
- Providing meeting space for Circles
- Active involvement in employee orientation and training
- Attend some Circle meetings
- Meet periodically with Leaders and Facilitators

Once upper management thoroughly understands and openly supports the Circle process, acceptance and implementation can be facilitated immeasurably. By allowing the workforce the opportunity to get involved in making decisions about their jobs, management is voicing support and commitment to participatory management concepts and believes that the workers do have something valuable to contribute to improve both themselves and the organization as a whole.

TRAINING

Training of the Company Facilitator is arranged. *The Company Facilitator trains the Leaders and the Departmental Facilitators selected by the Steering Committee.* Leaders and Facilitators are trained in extensive three to five day courses which include modules in problem prevention, identification, analysis, measurement techniques, and presentation skills used by the Circles, as well as training in group dynamics, motivation and communication skills.

The Leaders present the approach to the employees and request volunteers. It is important at this point to make sure the potential members are adequately oriented to Circle concepts so they can make an informed decision about future Quality Circle

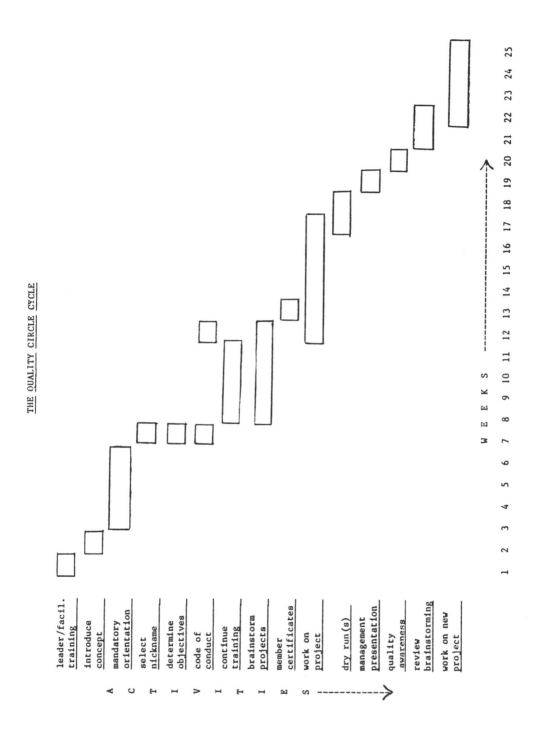

THE QUALITY CIRCLE CYCLE

leader/facil.
training

introduce
concept

A   mandatory
     orientation

C   select
     nickname

T   determine
     objectives

I   code of
     conduct

V   continue
I   training

T   brainstorm
I   projects

E   member
     certificates

S   work on
     project

     dry run(s)

     management
     presentation

     quality
     awareness

     review
     brainstorming

     work on new
     project

W E E K S ————————→

1 2 3 4 5 6 7 8 9 10 11 12 13 14 15 16 17 18 19 20 21 22 23 24 25

involvement. The more orientation the better, (e.g., two one-hour sessions as opposed to one half-an-hour).

Once potential members have decided to join, the Leader then trains the volunteers during Circle meetings in many useful and relevant problem-solving tools and measurement techniques. Typically, the Circles meet for one hour per week. This can be during regular working hours, overtime, or on the employees' own time, with or without pay, depending on what works best for each company. However, allowing meetings during working hours is evidence that management believes in and supports the process. The meeting agenda is divided with half of the time spent training Members, and half devoted to problem identification, analysis and recommendation.

The problem-solving and measurement techniques taught to Circle Members, Leaders, and Facilitators are varied. The new skills acquired through this instruction are useful both in problem-solving within Circle activities as well as for personal development outside the Circle. The tools and skills of project planning, brainstorming, data sampling, surveys, Pareto analysis, cause and effect analysis, flowcharting, work measurement, work simplification and project cost benefit analysis are the core modules taught to all involved in Quality Circle activities.

When Members receive sufficient training and become somewhat self-directing, assistance from and contact with the Facilitator declines. Occasional training refreshers are given by the Facilitator to keep the newly learned skills sharp.

RECOGNITION

A presentation to management, formal or informal, is given by the Leader and Circle Members when a recommendation is to be made. The Facilitator is usually present. The presentation is important because management is informed of Circle activities and accomplishments, and Circle Members are recognized for their contributions. Management response to the presentation is equally important. An estimated 80% of Circle recommendations are accepted and implemented in most companies. However, if a manager does not accept a proposal, it is essential that he/she explain the reasons for the rejection, and show support and enthusiasm for the Circle's efforts. Recognition and evaluation by the manager, positive or negative, is better than no response at all.

Once a decision on a presentation is made by a manager, the Circle can either select a new problem to work on or revise the former proposal if it was not accepted. Although the Facilitator is now spending less time with the Circle, the quality of their interactions should remain high. The Facilitator can assist the Circle in revising a rejected recommendation, finding a new direction, or lending moral support when an idea is rejected.

Many factors motivate the Quality Circle to continue working and growing. William H. Franklin, consultant and professor of Management at Georgia State University, makes four suggestions to help create a work place where positive performance is likely to occur. Managers of Quality Circle Members should keep these suggestions in mind when trying to show support for Circle efforts. First, make expectations abundantly clear; let the Circle know what can be done to make a recommendation more feasible or acceptable if it has been rejected. Second, deliver what you promise, don't promise what you can't personally deliver; follow up on

Objectives

The objectives set by those accepting the Quality Circle concept follow the philosophy closely:

- Reduction of errors
- Enhancement of quality
- Inspiration of more effective teamwork by co-workers
- Increased interaction of employees within sections and divisions
- Promotion of involvement in and commitment to the services provided to the customer
- Increased employee motivation to achieve high quality
- Development of problem-solving abilities, especially in the 1st-line employee
- Creation of a "problem prevention" attitude
- Improvement in communications between employees, at all levels
- Development of harmonious manager/employee relationships
- Promotion of personal and professional development
- Development of leadership potential of all employees
- Increased understanding of the importance of quality and the customer
- Promotion of cost consciousness

implementation for efforts which cannot be approved or arranged. Thirdly, give personal attention to all work; do not ignore Circle activities and efforts. Lastly, be a good model; show enthusiasm and pride in Circle projects.

The management presentation itself is the best example of how management can support Circle activities. Higher level management review and Circle management presentations to other departments or companies will provide the Circle with a unique and special form of recognition.

Public recognition through International Association of Quality Circles, *Quality Progress* or *Quality* Magazines, The American Banker, internal newspapers or newsletters, quarterly reports, office bulletins and division meetings can also be effective motivators. Publication of Circle progress in external publications adds prestige and esteem to Circle efforts.

The performance appraisal and salary administration systems, although not directly used to reward Circle involvement, can reflect an employee's personal growth through participation in a Quality Circle.

Material rewards, such as certificates or pins, can be important reminders to Members that their contributions to the organization are appreciated.

The recognition given to Quality Circle activities can be the single most significant factor in motivating Circle Members. Therefore, the ways in which the Circle will be recognized are important considerations for the Steering Committee.

MEASUREMENT

Measuring the results of Quality Circle activities is essential. Only scientifically and methodically gathered data will serve as evidence of success and appease skeptical critics. Measurement data also provides feedback to Quality Circles to effect changes and stimulate improvement. Both objective and subjective data can assist companies in evaluating their Quality Circle process.

There are numerous ways to track Circle effectiveness using objective information. Quality measures and standards programs can be implemented simultaneously, or preferably, prior to Circle initiation. These programs provide the necessary performance indices and defect rates to compare performances before and after implementing Quality Circles.

Tangible results can also be viewed from a financial perspective. Companies can easily determine their ROI by monitoring savings as a result of Circle Operation, compared to costs involved in the implementation and operation of Quality Circles. Payback ratios in companies where Quality Circles have been successfully implemented range from 2:1 to 8:1. R.J. Barra, coordinator of the Westinghouse program cautions, "If you emphasize the dollars and cents and make this a management program, it will die out, but if the people embrace it as their program, it can live forever."

Productivity, absenteeism, turnover, disciplinary orders, firings, hirings from within company ranks, and use of medical and counseling services are all variables which can be quantified and monitored, before and after implementation, and used as indicators of the implementation's success.

Records of Circle activities should be kept. These records provide case studies of what has been accomplished and how much was saved. They also serve as a foundation for Circle reports to senior level company officials. These reports can assimilate the recorded information for detailed analyses of the success or failure of the program.

Objective data is sometimes hard to obtain for rating Circle activities, and because of the qualitative nature of these activities, subjective measurement is equally necessary in order to determine the success of the program. As Howard Ferguson, manager of Quality Circles for the Westinghouse Defense and Electronics Systems Center stated, "The intangible results of increased employee job satisfaction, improved employee-management communication . . . are immeasurable objectively, but I feel the return is even greater than for tangible matters."

These intangible results can be measured through employee displays of increased quality consciousness, improved morale and communications, and increased interest in and attendance at Quality Circle meetings.

Perhaps the most empirical way of capturing this subjective data is by conducting attitude surveys. Asking direct questions, which are found to be methodically sound by test experts, can give much insight into the effectiveness of Quality Circles.

The importance of these attitudes was expressed by C.H. Molde, an operations vice president for one corporation, ". . . we don't just measure our success in terms of dollars saved or Circles in operation. More important factors to us are the way our working style has changed and the way productivity and quality of working life have improved in our division."

Other subjective measures, recognition and feedback from outside sources such as customer complaints, customer perception surveys and correspondence are also acceptable measures. The number of articles and presentations on the subject accepted or requested from outside publications or organizations is another measure of the success of Quality Circles.

QUALITY CIRCLES IN SERVICE INDUSTRIES

The industrial world embraced scientific management a generation ago. The business world was propelled forward with the adoption of related scientific techniques. Methodology such as quality control, industrial engineering, cost accounting and marketing research introduced empiricism into the business world. Likewise, an increasing number of growth-oriented service firms are taking major steps to apply parallel concepts, which they have adapted to the unique circumstances of each business to improve overall efficiency and profits.

The Quality Circles concept, a by-product of both the quality and behavioral sciences, is one technique which can be utilized in service industries. The organizational structure, operational model, and reliance on concrete results are empirical Quality Circle characteristics which readily lend themselves to use in service firms.

Although flexibility may be needed to integrate Quality Circles into predominantly white-collar situations, the approach has been attempted. The success of these Quality Circles has not been documented as extensively as it has been in other industries. However, this may be a result of the small proportion of Circles implemented in service fields, as compared to manufacturing.

Themes for Circle projects or specific problems to be solved may be more difficult to identify in service industries. If there is no specific common function, or work area, common problems may be hard to select. This is where the Steering Committee, managers or Facilitators may be able to make suggestions. The Leader must effectively and enthusiastically encourage creativity, and insure the use of brainstorming. Members should concentrate on those aspects of their functions which *are* similar. Equipment or forms used, services offered, or procedures may be starting points.

Some examples of large service companies who have initiated a Quality Circle program are Continental Bank, the Federal Aviation Administration, American Airlines, Sanwa Bank, Blue Cross Blue Shield, Bank of America, and Lincoln National Life Insurance. Although information regarding service Quality Circles is hard to locate, it can be conjected that the application will be successful if the manufacturing model is followed, with minimal modification.

Dr. J.M. Juran, foremost authority on Quality Circles, believes that Quality

Circles can work only, "if companies realize they're depriving themselves of using the abilities of a highly educated and creative workforce and use Circles as one way to turn that around."

POTENTIAL PROBLEMS

Quality Circles may not solve all problems. Many potential problems and real difficulties must be faced when installing the program, and management must be aware of them. Jeff Beardsley, a Quality Circles consultant, has outlined difficulties which may be encountered during implementation and operation:
- Working out details with existing suggestion systems or quality control programs
- Failure of previous programs
- Too much or too little publicity
- Impatience on the part of either management or the Circle Members
- Selecting problems which are too difficult for the Circle
- Scheduling problems
- Poor management response to the suggestions
- Failure to involve the peripheral organization

Additional potential problems include the following:
- Failure to emphasize technical aspects
- Not keeping management informed or involved
- Program grows too fast or too slow
- Inadequate Leader preparation
- Lack of visual management support
- Failure to keep Members informed of progress
- Starting to work on problems too soon
- Overemphasis on quick financial return or productivity increase

The potential problem of "Americanizing" Quality Circles has been an interesting issue. Many managers believe that Quality Circles cannot be successful in the United States, or at most, be as successful as Japanese Circles, due to the different motivational base fostered in Japan. For example, the Japanese worker views rework as a sign of failure. American industries have made a conservative estimate that 15% to 40% of productive capacity may be accounted for in rework and is generally accepted. According to R.E. Cole, director of the Center for Japanese Studies at the University of Michigan, "The big difference is that, almost out of necessity, the Japanese organizations have developed an environment that encourages worker contribution and participation." If this is indeed the "big difference," American companies need to provide work atmospheres which "create ... positive expectations."

Secondly, Americans recognize that the Japanese employment system nurtures company loyalty. Workers in Japan are frequently employed with one organization for a lifetime. Firms may reason that with such a loyalty lacking in American culture, Circles may fail. What these firms fail to realize or understand is that Quality Circles may be just the vehicle needed to encourage such company loyalty.

"We used to hear the objection that Quality Circles wouldn't work here because American employees are different from Japanese employees. We don't hear that anymore." Don Dewar concludes: "U.S. Quality Circles are working."

54

PLANNING AND IMPLEMENTATION

Once a decision had been made to adopt the Quality Circle process, an extensive planning stage begins. A complete understanding of the Quality Circle concept, philosophy, and application are necessary to assure effective implementation and operation. Having defined a Quality Circle and your objectives, you need the organization to basically understand and accept the process, and embrace the philosophy. This can be conducted through formal and informal interviews, discussion, and educational campaigns aimed at top management, middle management, and clerical level employees. Once top management has endorsed and supported the process, individual operating areas throughout the organization should be approached and given the option to start Circles on a pilot basis. If the manager has no interest in Circles, they should not be forced to participate.

The first step in the actual implementation process is the formation of a departmental Steering Committee for each of the areas participating in the process. The extensive size of an organization might make one interdepartmental Steering Committee both unfeasible and impractical. As an alternative, develop multiple Steering Committees to best gauge and assess the needs and characteristics of each unique area, one within each major department. The Steering Committees are composed of representatives from various management levels and functional areas to create a "diagonal slice" through the organizational chart. This cross-representation enables each section within a given division or department to play an active role in the policy-making process. Perhaps even more importantly, Steering Committee involvement and participation generates increased understanding of and support for the Quality Circle process. Steering Committees meet weekly initially, and gradually monthly, to develop Circle policies, procedures, and individual implementation and expansion plans. In addition, they also identify the pilot Circle Leaders (a work unit supervisor) and Facilitators (staff or line personnel).

Whereas Circle Leaders are always first-line supervisors, use of Facilitators is much more unique. Instead of several full-time Facilitators to oversee and coordinate the Circle process, have an expansive network of part-time Facilitators within each operating area. Part-time Facilitators are full-time employees who are trained in Circle techniques and given additional responsibilities for coordinating from one to five Circles. These Facilitators are usually staff personnel, but line management personnel have also been successfully utilized. Not only will this network enable rapid and effective expansion, but it will also keep program costs down while simultaneously developing these individuals in problem-solving and group skills.

The pilot Circle Leaders and part-time Facilitators can attend a three to five day in-house or outside training class. This training includes audio-visual problem-solving modules which introduce topics such as: project planning, brainstorming, sampling, surveying, flowcharting, work measurement, work simplification, Pareto analysis, cause and effect analysis, and project cost benefit analysis. On the behavioral side, motivation, group dynamics, and communication skills are introduced and practiced by the trainees. As the Circles mature and advance, new problem-solving skills and tools can be introduced to continue employee development and further maximize the problem-solving capabilities of your Circles.

Concurrent with the Leader/Facilitator training, hold an extensive management orientation and training program to expose all levels of management to the Circle concept. Managers should receive a full day training session on the Circle concept in general as well as the problem-solving techniques. Middle managers should be given a day and a half training in Circle concepts and techniques with specific emphasis on the role of middle management in the Circle process. In addition to familiarizing middle management with Circle philosophy, a major portion of this training is devoted to alleviating middle management fears and concerns about loss of control, resistance to change, production loss, etc. As a result of these seminars, management has a more accurate and thorough understanding of the Circle process in general, and their role in particular. They will be more committed to the Circle process and become more directly involved with their Circles through attendance at meetings, input into projects, provision of resources, and by recognizing Circle activities and presentations with enthusiasm, interest and praise. Management's visible involvement and active participation will not only provide valuable direction to the Circles, but also alleviate some of management's fear, resistance, and hostility towards the Circle concept.

Once management is adequately informed and the pilot Leaders/Facilitators trained, the next step is to solicit Members. A Member orientation and training session entails a thorough introduction of Quality Circle techniques prior to soliciting volunteers. Before potential Members have the opportunity to volunteer, all personnel in the area are expected to attend two to four hours of weekly one hour Circle meetings. After completing this orientation, the employees are given the option to join, and the remaining volunteers are then trained in the remaining Circle techniques or modules. This extensive Member orientation and training process provides potential Members with the ability to make an informed decision about their future Circle involvement. Furthermore, even if some employees opt not to join, at least they were exposed to basic problem-solving techniques (i.e., project planning, brainstorming, sampling) and could apply them independent of the Circle.

OPERATION

The operation of a Quality Circle is an ongoing cycle involving continued training in the problem-solving techniques, project identification, selection, analysis, and solution, culminating in a management presentation. The duration of Member training (including the orientation sessions) is usually between eight to 12 weeks depending on the level of the group as well as any other miscellaneous items covered during the training process (i.e., group name, code of conduct, communication exercises, etc.). The project cycle, (including selection, analysis, and presentation) was generally completed within the recommended four-month period. Even first projects, which tend to take longer, were usually completed in that time frame.

The entire Member training process is conducted by the Leader with the Facilitator providing guidance and technical expertise when needed. During the weekly one-hour meetings, Members are instructed in the techniques for one-half of the meeting. The remainder is devoted to applying the concepts to a generic or work-related example.

The successful completion of training is followed by project identification and selection. The majority of Circles are composed of employees from the same work area, or performing the same functional tasks. In this way, all Members of the group are familiar enough with the work to focus on common work-related issues. Although any interested employee, staff person, or manager can suggest topics, the ultimate selection of a project is actually done by the Circle Members. Once the project is selected, Members begin the process by first planning the project then gathering the information through surveys and sampling. Then they analyze it through the use of techniques such as Pareto analysis, work simplification, work measurement, cause and effect analysis, flow charting, and various other techniques as applicable. The Members then brainstorm for solution alternatives, test the recommendations, prepare a cost benefit analysis and prepare for the management presentation.

Despite the fact that the Circles recommend solutions and suggested courses of action, the appropriate level of management still retains the authority for the final decision. In general, the management presentations are consistently thorough, of high quality, and professional in both content and style. Furthermore, a majority of the projects involve improvements in the work itself (i.e., quality and productivity enhancements) as opposed to "cosmetic" changes. The management presentation itself, as well as a high acceptance rate, generate renewed enthusiasm from the Circle Members and motivate them to continue their problem-solving efforts. In addition, as active participants in developing work-related improvements and seeing the results, Members are more committed to following through on proposed changes and maintaining a high level of quality in their work area.

Throughout the operation phase, communication and attitude improvements will be noticed on all levels. Leader/Facilitator luncheons are offered on a quarterly basis to recognize Leaders and Facilitators for successfully completing their training. Upper and middle management representatives attend these quarterly luncheons to show their support and directly interact with the Leaders and Facilitators on the subject of Quality Circles. Facilitators in the larger departments meet on a bimonthly basis to discuss relevant Circle issues and concerns. These meetings identify additional training needs and serve as an important link between the Steering Committees and the Circles. Leader meetings are established on a quarterly basis to provide supervisors with a structured forum to discuss and assess Circle activities from a Leader perspective. In addition, quarterly reviews between Facilitators, Leaders, and management become a common activity. As a result of the open communication channels on and between the various levels, managers and management become even more directly involved in Circle activities. They attend many meetings and receive weekly Circle minutes which enable them to provide guidance, support, and resources to the Circles when needed. Management's genuine open, visible, and available support stimulates Member involvement and enthusiasm, and contributes greatly to the successful completion of projects.

RESULTS

The results of any Circle effort can be divided into two categories: intangible (people-building) and tangible (directly measurable) benefits. Gains in areas such as:

quality, productivity, customer service, employee attitudes, as well as savings can be achieved. Individual Circles and Leaders together with technical and staff experts are responsible for measuring and reporting the results of their Circle activities on a monthly basis. These results should be audited and monitored.

In terms of intangible or people-building benefits, the Circle process results in tremendous personal growth and development on all levels. One of the major advancements is the increased development of the Members, Leaders, Facilitators, and management in communication and interpersonal skills. The Circles provide employees with direct interaction with middle and upper management. This interaction occurs primarily at Circle meetings and management presentations. As a result of these structured communication vehicles, management and the Circle Members develop an increased understanding of each other on both a personal and professional level. Teamwork is enhanced as Circle Members develop better interpersonal and working relationships with their co-workers. Leaders and Facilitators are able to profit from regular meetings to discuss Circle activities. These meetings also expand the communication and support network between supervisors, staff personnel, and middle management as well. Lastly, the Steering Committee meetings further stimulate increased interaction and rapport between management levels as well as a more participative management style and approach.

A second major positive intangible benefit is management's increased awareness and acknowledgement of the untapped potential within the workforce. Many skills and talents emerge through Circles that would otherwise have been disregarded. Artistic, creative, and innate leadership abilities are recognized and reinforced through promotions, and Members rotating the leadership role. Leaders and Facilitators gain valuable experience in leading groups and managing people in a way which was never available to them previously. As a result of their Circle involvement, many Leaders become more effective supervisors through the use of participative techniques.

Through the Circle process, Members gain additional knowledge and insight into their own jobs and work units. In some areas where the work is monotonous, specialized, and isolated, the Circles provide Members with a broader framework from which to understand how their jobs impact the section, division, and their financial institution. This increased job knowledge heightens awareness of the importance of the customer and the necessity for high quality services. Overall, these intangible benefits improve the attitude and morale of the workforce. The development, training, and recognition received through Circle involvement reinforces Members' sense of accomplishment and personal value. This increased satisfaction and motivation, in turn, will be reflected in decreased absenteeism and turnover in areas where Circles have been implemented.

Although primary emphasis is on the development of people, empirical measurement of intangibles is difficult. Therefore, a comprehensive tangible measurement program is crucial in assuring the intangibles are being achieved as well as in maximizing management's continued support. One way to measure the tangible results of the Circle process is in terms of the number and types of Circles, and the participation rates. Furthermore, implementation of professional and management Circles, in addition to the clerical Circles, will broaden the application of the Quality Circle concept.

The quantity and quality of completed Circle projects is another tangible

Benefits

- **Greater sense of pride and interest in work**

- **Increased quality**

- **Increased productivity**

- **Decreased absenteeism and turnover**

- **Improved customer service to corporate customers**

- **Increased capability to hire from within and to develop employee potential**

- **Reduction in costs**

measurement of Circle effectiveness. Every time a project is completed, it is assigned to one of four categories: improved quality, increased productivity, improved work environment, or improved customer service. Although a project may fall into more than one category, it is assigned to the primary benefit category. A breakdown of these categories will clearly illustrate that a vast majority of Circle projects contribute to quality, productivity, and service as opposed to improving the physical work environment. And perhaps most importantly from a management perspective are the bottom line figures, the total cost savings accumulated from these projects.

Tremendous improvements in measurable quality, productivity, and customer service accrue for those areas participating in the Circle process. However, it must be recognized that these additional measures are indirect and may be affected by other programs and factors. Nonetheless, Quality Circles will contribute significantly to these findings and a noticeable performance jump should occur in areas with Circles within six months after implementation.

PARTICIPATIVE VS. AUTHORITATIVE MANAGEMENT

Once a total organization commits itself to the Quality Circle philosophy and process, the internal "consultant" may not be able to decline implementation in areas that are not assessed as "ready." Even after initiating readiness activities or programs (i.e., attitude or climate surveys, management training in accepting change, participative management and changing work values, Leader/Facilitator training, etc.), the ideal environment may still not exist. Nonetheless, the employees, management, and/or the organization may still demand implementation.

Despite the fact that the Circle process is generally consistent throughout the organization, there are nonetheless differences in Circle implementation, operation, and results between areas where management styles tend to be either authoritarian or participative. By authoritarian, we generally mean an autocratic and/or benevolent style, leaning toward McGregor's Theory X management philosophy, with a heavy task or production orientation. By participative, we are referring to a consultative, interactive style, tending toward McGregor's Theory Y philosophy, with a more people-oriented approach to management.

There are factors in the respective areas that tend to foster each style. The work in the more participative areas tends to be more technical in nature than in the authoritative areas. Due to the technical nature of the work, employees in the participative areas are at higher salary levels and are generally better educated. In contrast, employees in the authoritative areas are at lower salary levels, less educated, and the workforce consists of many more part-time employees. The majority of supervisors (Leaders) in the participative areas are college graduates whereas supervisors in the authoritative environments frequently worked their way up through the ranks. Furthermore, supervisors in the authoritative areas are directly responsible for an average of 30 people as compared to 15 in the participative areas. In addition, participative environments generally employ more staff support personnel and have more management layers than the authoritative areas. The volume of work and deadlines in the two areas also differ. Although participative areas do have a high volume of work (thousands/day) and daily deadlines, they are significantly less than in the authoritative environments (tens of thousands/day) and hourly deadlines. All of the above mentioned factors together with the management style, impact the implementation, operation, and results of a Quality Circle effort. However, the Quality Circle approach is assessed as beneficial and worthwhile in both areas.

IMPLEMENTATION DIFFERENCES

The major differences that will be encountered during implementation between the two environments will be the extent of management support, and initial orientation and training. In general, areas with a predominantly participative management philosophy have extremely strong and supportive upper management involvement which extends throughout all levels of the department. Support for the Quality Circle concept is communicated through both verbal endorsement and active participation. Conversely, in the authoritative areas, management is not as accepting and supportive of the Circle concept. In authoritative environments, management on all levels is extremely skeptical about the applicability of Circles in such a high

Quality Circle Project Benefits

Year	Total		
1983	54		Project acceptance rate: 98%
1984	119		

Total: 173(100%)

Year	Quality	Productivity	Work Area	Service	Savings
1983	17	15	7	15	$61,500
1984	33	40	16	30	$166,445
Total	**50** (29%)	**55** (32%)	**23** (13%)	**45** (26%)	**$227,945**

Circles

December 31, 1984

Area	Circles	Facilitators Leaders	Members	Participation Rate
Bond Operations	4	6	29	59%
Charge Card Operations	9	12	71	76%
Check Proc. Operations	38	93	239	49%
Controllers	7	9	45	73%
GBS Operations	81	114	535	59%
General Services	2	6	13	65%
Management Services	4	13	32	100%
Personnel	2	5	16	84%
Systems	2	4	18	100%
Total:	**149**	**262**	**998**	**59%**

productive and predominantly clerical level environment. Upper management initially endorses the Circle concept and communicates their commitment to the middle management level. Unfortunately, upper management's role diminishes considerably in terms of both visibility and active participation. Responsibility for Circle activities is delegated to middle managers who neither fully understand nor support the process.

The extent of initial orientation and training on the management level also varies considerably between the two environments. In the participative areas, all managers receive a full day training session on the Circle concept as well as the specific problem-solving techniques. Middle managers are given a day and a half training in Circle concepts and techniques with specific emphasis on the role of middle management in the Circle process. By exposing all levels of management to Quality Circle theory and giving them the opportunity to express their fears and concerns, management in the participative areas feels more committed to and directly involved with the future success of the Circles.

Unlike the participative areas, many authoritative environments do not provide adequate management orientation training sessions. Initial orientation sessions are provided to the Steering Committee, the Leaders, Facilitators, and Members, but unfortunately middle management neglects the training process. Although efforts are made to institute a comprehensive training program specifically emphasizing the role of middle management, these efforts are consistently unsuccessful until midway through the operation phase. As in many programs, management's own lack of insight into the underlying Circle concept and its associated benefits make it extremely difficult for them to provide assistance or support to their Circle Leaders, Facilitators and Members. Perhaps if middle management in the authoritative areas would be initially oriented, some of their resentment and fear could be reduced, and ultimately transformed into more constructive and beneficial channels.

OPERATIONAL DIFFERENCES

Monitoring Circle activities during the operation phase results in finding that participative areas tend to complete both training and projects more quickly and have better quality presentations. In most participative areas, despite discrepancies in grade levels, the training process is nonetheless completed within the recommended eight to twelve week period (averaging ten weeks). By the time these Circles begin brainstorming projects, they have already experienced a sense of personal pride and accomplishment for completing training and mastering the problem-solving techniques. Although in most cases the analysis, solution, recommendation, and presentation aspects of the Circle are foreign, the majority of Circles in the participative areas complete and give a management presentation within the suggested four month period. Furthermore, these projects focus primarily on quality, productivity, and service enhancements as opposed to environmental improvements. In many ways, Circle involvement in participative areas closely parallels their natural work environment; in the workplace, supervisors encourage and reward creative thinking, participation in decision-making, and responsibility for locating inefficiencies in the work process. Consequently, the identification, selection, and completion of a Circle project is accomplished with relative ease.

The authoritative areas, on the other hand, have a much rougher time during the operation phase. The training process itself lasts as long as four to five months, compared to eight to 12 weeks in the participative areas. One major interference throughout the training and project phase is the environmental pressures under which the Circles work. Due to the high volume of work, peak volume periods and constant deadlines, the Circles have difficulty in establishing and maintaining weekly one-hour meetings. Meetings are cancelled constantly under the guise of "heavy work flow" and are rarely rescheduled within five working days. A second factor which is perhaps even more damaging to the Circles' progress is related to the Members' skill level. In an environment where personal creativity, innovation, and initiative are not solicited, the Members are never given the opportunity to express themselves prior to the introduction of Circles. Once they are offered the chance to excel and improve the work, they didn't know what to do with it. The Members are unable or unwilling to take the initiative or responsibility necessary for an effective Circle. This lengthy and extensive training period serves to inhibit the Circle process and results in many Circle dropouts.

The project phase in authoritative areas is lengthy and tedious, averaging six to seven months per project. Circle Members have very limited knowledge of their work area so they have difficulty identifying potential projects. Despite attempts by the Leaders and Facilitators to guide the groups toward appropriate and meaningful projects, the Circles usually choose projects which are either outside their area of expertise, are already being worked on by management, or are so insignificant that they are meaningless. Once the Circles succeed in picking a project, they have an equally difficult time applying the Circle techniques to collect and analyze data. The solutions or recommendations are usually fairly evident and straight-forward. Most authoritative Circles are not very creative in their approach, not wanting to "shake the boat." The actual presentations however, are usually professional, well-organized, and of high quality. The major flaw running throughout many of them is a lack of specific follow-up or implementation plans.

DIVERGENT RESULTS

Positive and worthwhile results are obtained in both areas, although the magnitude and types of benefits differ significantly. One interesting observation is that tangible results such as quality, productivity, and cost savings are more frequent in the participative areas despite management's emphasis on people-building. On the other hand, the authoritative areas view intangible gains as secondary to the more quantitative benefits, yet the majority of improvements occur in the areas they least expect or desire. In terms of intangible or people-building elements, the Circle processes in participative areas formalize and expand on management and employee development practices which were essentially already in existence prior to Circles. The authoritative environments also realize people-building benefits. In some senses, these intangible accomplishments are even more salient in the authoritative areas because they are a total departure from previous practices. Both environments nonetheless achieve significant improvements in teamwork, communication, job awareness, and personal recognition.

Success Factors

- **Genuine management support**
- **Leader commitment/enthusiasm**
- **Member accomplishment**
- **Valuable results**
- **Review and assessment**

The major difference in results between the two environments occur in the quantity and quality of tangible or measurable benefits. The participative areas have a consistently positive increase in the number of Circles and participation rates while Circles in the authoritative areas fluctuate dramatically and ultimately develop a downward participation rate. In terms of Circle projects, the majority of Circles in the participative areas deal with the work itself which results in quality, productivity, and cost savings benefits. On the other hand, Circle projects in the more authoritative areas work on environmental and hygiene factors which do not usually provide bottom line paybacks. In addition, as mentioned previously, authoritative areas take twice as long as the participative areas to complete projects.

Further analysis of tangible results between the two areas can be provided by examining customer service reports, quality performance, and productivity measurements. Customer service data for both areas is compiled on average turnaround time for investigations and percent of service volume in error affecting the customer. Although the net percentage decrease is greater for the authoritative environments, the absolute values (days) are lower in the participative areas to begin with. In addition, even though there is no net change in percent of service volume in error for participative areas, authoritative areas increase the percent of service volume in error by 11% (negative trend) for the same time period.

Improvements in quality performance and productivity can also be noted. Both environments' quality conformance to standard increase in excess of 10%, with the authoritative areas improving slightly more than that. In terms of service defect rates, participative areas increase defects while authoritative areas decrease slightly. Productivity measurements demonstrate that authoritative environments' productivity trends improve while participative environments' productivity trends decrease. However, part of the decreasing productivity trend in participative areas is a result of changing the base measurement which negatively impacts the service defect rate and productivity numbers. Although the authoritative environments accrue greater quality and productivity benefits overall, the major contributors to these improvements possibly result from other programs already in existence prior to the introduction of Circles.

The comparison of Circles in authoritative versus participative environments is quite enlightening. The major differences during implementation are the extent of management support as well as the amount of initial orientation and training, particularly on the management level. During the operation phase, authoritative areas take twice as long to complete training and projects, compared to participative areas who complete training and projects in a concise, thorough and systematic fashion. Furthermore, the participative areas complete more projects, which are more effective, and result in greater cost savings. Authoritative areas, on the other hand, complete fewer projects, and these primarily contribute to work area or environmental factors as opposed to quality or productivity. But perhaps even more importantly, the authoritarian management group is moving, albeit slowly, to a more participative style. So despite differences in the magnitude and types of results in the two environments, both Circle programs are nonetheless assessed as positive, beneficial, and worthwhile.

CHAPTER V

Motivating High Quality Performance

Incentives provide motivation to do what is required, and to do it effectively. Both financial and nonfinancial incentives help achieve and maintain high levels of productivity and quality. Any enterprise that needs to create an environment conducive to motivating employees to behave in a way not of their own choosing must consider incentives.

There are two distinctly different ways to motivate employees. These include positive motivators in which an employee is rewarded for achievement, and negative incentives whereby an employee is penalized for failure to achieve.

Negative incentives usually take the form of such corrective actions as no salary increase, bonus, or promotion for a poor performer. While this might seem harsh to that individual employee, negative incentives serve as a standard of fairness for all other employees.

Positive incentives include both financial and nonfinancial types. Nonfinancial motivators deal with the work environment—the nature of the company work, the status and security of a job, employee treatment, and the image of the business in the eyes of employees.

A great deal more concrete and observable experience has been gained with respect to financial incentives. A company's salary increase system can financially motivate employees by either promotion increases or true merit increases. Promotional pay increases occur when employees are promoted to distinctly higher positions or achieve a new level of professional competency with added responsibilities. On the other hand, merit-increase programs are based on the notion that employees whose performance is bettered should receive more money since improved performance means greater productivity.

The newest development in incentive-pay compensation plans applies to middle-group employees where three types of plans have successfully evolved. In the goal-oriented plan, performance criteria are created and higher and lower goals are met. Discretionary plans provide certain individuals with the discretion and authority to develop specific performance criteria, the methods of measuring performance, and the pay system for awarding individual work contributions. The special award plan rewards those who have, according to their supervisors, made extraordinary achievements in their jobs during the year.

Contrary to incentives, disincentives are financial and nonfinancial plans that motivate employees to violate standards, avoid the system, work effectively on the wrong things, or work by the wrong methods. Disincentives must be identified and removed before steps are taken to adopt positive incentives.

It is difficult to establish precisely, the actual improvement in productivity resulting from the implementation of incentive plans. Still, almost all management people in companies that have incentive plans believe such incentive programs make a positive contribution toward more effective employee work. And employees themselves generally favor incentive pay plans because they believe they will earn more money. Ideally, under an incentive pay plan, the better performers are the better paid employees.

INCENTIVES

What motivates employees? What makes workers perform to the best of their ability? The subject of incentives provokes such questions and knowing the answers as they apply to individual employees or to groups of employees, is essential in effective management of human resources. Studies examining the incentives issue reveal a number of interesting points. First, there is never, or almost never, a single factor which motivates people. Secondly, for most people, money is the number one motivator during most of their work career. Thirdly, people tend to be motivated to obtain things which they do not have or do not think they have. For example, employees in low paying jobs place money on the top of their priority list while people in insecure positions tend to value security relatively higher than do those in very stable work environments.

Incentives provide motivation to do what is required, and to do it effectively. Both financial and nonfinancial incentives are critical parts of a management system's approach toward achieving and maintaining high levels of productivity and quality. There is a direct and frequently measurable relationship between many incentive programs and the productivity of workers. Consequently, any enterprise that needs to create an environment conducive to motivating employees to behave in a way not of their own choosing must consider incentives.

Incentives alone, of course, will not bring about higher productivity or a higher quality product. Some companies have erred in the past by relying solely on the power of incentives to obtain these increasing levels. On the other hand, it is equally incorrect to assume that there could be an effective work force or a higher level of productivity or even a quality product without having some type of incentives.

Experience proves that incentives should be applicable to all employees of an organization and should only be implemented in the context of a firm's overall motivational system. A great number of different incentive plans are available and appropriate for different levels of employees. In light of any overall motivational system, nonfinancial matters for employees, such as job security and the general work environment must be considered. Positive and negative incentives, along with the removal of deterrents must also be remembered. Finally, the overall motivational system must include financial incentives consisting of promotion, pay practices and performance salary increases.

Another vital consideration of all incentives is cost. Incentives usually involve time costs and some expenditures of money which create a cost/value variable in the management of incentives. The enterprise goal is to have the value or return from incentive plans exceed the cost of such plans. Thus, the structuring of incentives must represent the appropriate balancing of motivating people to work at optimum effort on the right job at a cost that justifies improvement in operations.

It has been said that some people will work just as well without incentives as they would with them. Usually, such views are expressed when a company is contemplating supplementary incentive pay plans. Frequently, these views, are very personal and moralistic—good people don't need incentives. The assumption is that employees don't respond to motivation. This anti-incentive notion reflects a serious lack of knowledge with regard to the instinctive human qualities of the average employee, as demonstrated by psychological research.

When developing incentive plans, it is critical to keep in mind that the objective of incentives is to induce employees to extend proper and reasonable effort. It is not to get hard working employees to work harder. Effort itself needs to be defined if work (input) and value (output) are to be analyzed. Effort may be interpreted as partly elapsed time or hours at work, which to employees usually means hours on the job, although sometimes employees perceive it as hours away from home. Effort may also mean hours working, as opposed to hours at work, or may mean how much energy is expended while working. Therefore, incentives influence both the amount of time employees spend working and how much effort they expend while working.

Still, effective work in any enterprise means far more than just hours or effort. Faster motion or more frenzied movement does not necessarily mean more effective work. Productivity also depends on the employee's willingness to do things in a positive way, which they would otherwise choose not to do, not think to do, and occasionally, dislike doing. In this way, incentives represent a business expression of the psychological concept of stimuli. As long as people seek more in the way of material rewards and higher standards of living, compensation incentives will play a key role in the overall stimuli necessary for obtaining full utilization of human resources.

In operations work, studies show that incentive plans affect productivity dramatically. Under incentive plans, productivity is typically 20 percent higher and in some cases employee productivity has doubled when an incentive plan was implemented. Nevertheless, incentives don't always show such dramatic results in a short period of time. Instead, studies of plans covering top management and professional employees have found that changes in behavior and increased effectiveness typically occur gradually over time. Sometimes they result only in a small increase of 5 to 10 percent in productivity. Yet, the leverage effect of a 10 percent increase has considerable influence on effectiveness of work in the enterprise.

At the same time, there is a limit to how hard employees can work or should work. If employees perceive that the incentives are forcing them to work beyond reasonable limits, then the incentive system will have a negative effect. It could possibly motivate people to work hard to loosen up on standards or to take shortcuts in the system. Incentives, as a part of the management of human resources, aims at a delicate balance between employee effort and work expectations. There is a general relationship between hours at work plus effort expended during those hours on the one hand, and output on the other. There is also a level of input which represents inadequate input. Most employees are likely to choose a level of effort that falls in the range of inadequacy. Incentives, in part, motivate employees to expend greater effort and work at an optimum level of effort. Once employees get used to this optimum level of effort, most find it more satisfying than an inadequate work pace.

Incentives must not though, motivate employees to expend effort beyond the optimum level. If they do, the work pace and effort becomes physically and emotionally overdemanding, and only incremental increases in output occur.

This is the high-risk level of effort that is distasteful and perhaps harmful to employees, while of marginal value to the enterprise. Additional effort is excessive as most employees cannot endure such a pace except for very short periods of time, after which total output declines.

Besides working harder, properly structured incentives can motivate people to work smarter as well. Such incentives allow employees to order their priorities properly, focus on the important work, and follow the most effective methods. This purpose of incentives is particularly important in worker-controlled production, which is becoming common in an increasing number of jobs. All those jobs that apply technical or professional knowledge in areas that may not be methodized or institutionalized, where output cannot be quantified, and where the concept of "productiveness" is crucial to work effectiveness, contain worker-controlled production. Even a growing number of service industry jobs have one or more of these characteristics.

NEGATIVE INCENTIVES

In a broad sense, there are two distinctly different ways to motivate employees. Namely, positive motivators such as financial incentives whereby an employee is rewarded for achievement, and negative incentives whereby an employee is penalized for failure to achieve. Ideally, a company should always strive to build nothing but positive incentives, yet as a practical matter, negative incentives are to some extent a necessary part of every overall motivational system.

Negative incentives describe forms of fear or concern for loss of job, down grading, and other punitive personal actions. Since the blatant use of power is unacceptable social behavior for business, negative incentives must be implemented with caution. Actions by the enterprise which represents arbitrary discipline or improper use of authority incites reactions from employees, either as individuals or in groups. Most assuredly then, the company that operates under a constant environment of confrontation is not a very productive enterprise.

However, the use of negative incentives need not be punitive. In fact, they are more appropriately structured as being corrective. Corrective personal actions may serve as passive negative incentives when poorer performers get more moderate salary increases or no salary increases at all, when their bonus awards are small or zero, or when they are not considered for promotional opportunities. To be effective, a corrective approach towards negative incentives must be accompanied by effective communication. Employees must know what is expected in the first place, and they must be told how they failed to accomplish what was expected. If employees are to perceive these actions as fair treatment, they must receive assistance from the supervisor in correcting deficiencies.

In the same way, negative incentives must not be so strong that they create an environment of fear. This may retroact and motivate people to be ultra-conservative so that they lose the incentive to try. Stringent negative incentives also discourage the important inclination of persons to take unpopular positions on issues which experience may later prove were correct and in the vital interest of the firm.

While negative incentives may appear to be inherently disagreeable, they do serve a positive purpose. Corrective action with respect to an employee who is not measuring up, or who performs in an inappropriate fashion, may seem harsh to that individual, but it is the essence of fairness to other employees. Inappropriate action by one employee detracts from job opportunities and the work environment of others. Management, of course, must take the enterprise point of view and represent the interests and asipirations of the majority of employees, guarding against any inequities.

NONFINANCIAL INCENTIVES

Very often, consideration of incentives is narrowly viewed as only financial incentive plans and pay practices. Even though they are less reliable, nonfinancial incentives play a significant role in any firm's overall motivational system. Especially from a cumulative perspective, nonfinancial incentives are an extremely important segment of a company's motivational system.

Primarily, nonfinancial incentives deal with the environment of work. The elements representing nonfinancial incentives include the physical work environment, the nature of the company work, and the image of the business in the eyes of employees. Even such work environmental characteristics as the expectations for excellence represent a form of nonfinancial incentive.

Certainly, a job itself can be an important nonfinancial incentive. It is generally true that people work harder, more diligently, and with more enthusiasm when they are performing tasks they enjoy. For some then, whether or not the job is interesting and diverse can be an incentive while conversely, the degree to which the job is routine and uninteresting represents a nonfinancial incentive for others who prefer less taxing work.

The manner in which employees are treated by their supervisors and coworkers is a determinant of job satisfaction and therefore, a nonfinancial incentive. Such employee treatment consists of how instructions are given, daily treatment by supervisors, and how much assistance a supervisor provides to employees. It also includes how well an employee's questions are answered or how well grievances are resolved. The quality of supervision and the role of the human-resources unit manager powerfully influences the effectiveness of nonfinancial incentives.

At different stages in their careers, many employees are far more motivated toward broadening their knowledge and increasing their personal asset values then they are in moving ahead. For these workers, the degree to which their job represents a learning experience can be a nonfinancial motivator that determines employee satisfaction.

Employee satisfaction is also indicated by job security and the level of self esteem established by a job. Hence, both these factors act simultaneously as nonfinancial incentives for many people.

Furthermore, the status of a job and the recognition that is given to its occupant serves as an element of nonfinancial incentives. Companies are constantly dealing with the problems of title, office location, parking lot priorities, etc. Each of these elements may seem minor when considered separately, but when combined together, these benefits exert a significant influence over an employee's attitudes and the effectiveness of his work.

Some of these nonfinancial incentives are "givens" and are not manageable. For example, a company cannot change its business in order to create more favorable nonfinancial incentives, nor can it tailor side benefits to fit the view of the recipients. Status may be very important to one person, but embarrassing to another. Some people may covet security strongly, while others consider it demeaning to be concerned about security.

Unfortunately, the cause-and-effect relationships between nonfinancial incentives and productivity are very obscure and unclear. There has been enough evidence to indicate that these relationships are real and cumulatively important. They cannot, however, be quantified, and it is very difficult to find a measuring stick that is able to pinpoint their effectiveness.

Worse yet, some nonfinancial incentives can become disincentives. Titles and other symptoms of stature serve well to illustrate this transformation. If overemphasized, employees can strive for the trappings of success rather than the substance of success. They work hard and structure their thinking and activities to seem important, but they do not work efficiently. Hence, the management of nonfinancial incentives as a means to gaining greater productivity is a tenuous task that demands a keen sensitivity to differences in people.

FINANCIAL INCENTIVES

A great deal more concrete and observable experience has been gained with respect to financial incentives than to nonfinancial incentives. Much of this experience can be generalized to provide ground rules for evaluating financial incentives at every level. Some of these rules are:

> Employees must know what the goals are and what the rewards are. This means that they must know exactly what comprises the performance criteria area, and what measurement system is used. This information must be available before the start of each planned period.

> The goals must be understandable. This means that the performance criteria must relate not only to things that employees perceive and understand, but must also be clear enough so that those covered by the plan are well aware of how that plan works.

> The goals must be attainable. This, of course, means that they must be attainable in the eyes of the employees as well as in the eyes of management.

> There must be a very distinct and direct relationship between what an individual accomplishes, or what a group of employees accomplish, and the rewards they receive.

> The reward must be significant. In other words, the race must be worth the running.

There must be a reasonably short time span between recognition of employee accomplishments and the time the rewards are received.

The reward must be irrevocable. It must not be subject to future jeopardy.

An employee must have the tools or the facilities to accomplish work expectations.

The incentive system cannot be in conflict with other vital employee interests. It may not, for instance, be in conflict with the basic security needs of employees.

The financial incentive system must be compatible with the overall job requirements, work environment, and the general management style of the firm.

SALARY INCREASE SYSTEM

Before considering extra compensation systems as a form of financial incentives, a company would be well advised to first pay attention to its basic salary administration system. Financial incentives can only be built into the company's practice after a sound salary administration has been established. Otherwise, extra-compensation incentive plans super-imposed on chaotic salary administration can result in greater chaos and possible disproductivity. Once a company is prepared to initiate an extra compensation system, employees can be financially motivated by either promotion increases or true merit increases.

PROMOTIONAL PAY INCREASES

Almost all companies grant salary increases to their employees when they are promoted to distinctly higher positions. To be effective, the promotion increase must be immediate and significant. Certainly, the employee must do better financially after the promotion than the increases he or she would have received without being promoted. Companies must also deal with promotional increases for those employees, such as professional employees, who do not experience promotions by going from one job to a distinctly different job, but rather get "promoted" because they achieve a new level of professional competency or because they have received added responsibilities.

Most companies have mastered the rather simplistic problems of promotional pay increases. Particularly in rapidly growing companies, these can represent extremely effective and strong financial incentives. In one of the most successful growth companies today, International Business Machines, exempt employees in the past five years received a promotion and a promotional increase on the average of every 15 months. While the frequency and size of these promotional increases do indeed reflect strong financial incentives, IBM would say that it has no financial incentive plan per se; even though the average salary increase, compounded annually, exceeded 18 percent for all of its employees during the period of study.

MERIT PAY INCREASES

With merit pay increases, companies have had far greater difficulties in creating salary incentives. The traditional merit-increase concept advocates that employees whose performance is stronger should receive larger increases and should receive more money for a given job. The theory is that if we pay people more for better performance, their productivity will increase. And if productivity increases, business results will be improved.

Unfortunately, most merit-increase programs have never fulfilled this objective. From the very beginning, salary administrators find problems of measurement. How do we determine through performance appraisal or merit rating who is performing better and how much better? First attempts at measurement are made by identifying traits of behavior, such as attitude, education, and experience. The measurements are then improved to develop more direct measures of performance on the job, including the identification of critical success factors, the setting of standards of performance, and the evaluation of achievement in relation to goals or objectives. But even here, the task of developing forms and systems that will collect information about performance, which can be the basis for salary increases, along with transmitting this information to some central point, presents insurmountable problems.

Secondly, many merit-increase programs incorrectly assume that the sole criteria for granting salary increases should be the performance of individuals. Actually, salary increases must reflect a number of important considerations besides performance. These considerations include the change in the cost of living, pay parity with other employees, (particularly those covered by union contracts), and pay relationships between employees.

In order to combat such measurement problems, some companies have recently introduced a new generation of effective merit-increase programs. These problems still exist though, because designers of salary systems are still pursuing the idea of some central point for information that is already known locally.

One of the fundamental features of the new merit-increase programs is conclusions appraisal. By implementing conclusions appraisal, supervisors at the unit, section, or location level can identify the outstanding performers, the marginal performers, and the intermediate-level performers. A number of tests have clearly demonstrated that people who have observed the performance of a sample group can rate performance with fair accuracy. These conclusions ratings are all that is needed for approving or disapproving performance salary increase.

A second key feature of the new generation of merit-increase programs is the recognition of the basic limitations of the conclusions performance appraisal mentioned above. First of all, it is not possible at most job levels to make more than five distinctions with respect to performance. Human judgment is simply not capable of pinpointing more discrete distinctions with respect to observable work performance. Therefore, if discrete distinctions in excess of five gradients are indicated, they reflect something other than performance.

In terms of practicalities of salary administration, this means that salary increases granted for improved performance may not be less than about 7 or 8 percent annually. Specifically, a salary increase for performance must be in the range of 7, 8, 14, 21 percent, etc. Of course there may be small variations in this scale, but certainly no single individual should be granted an increase of one percent in recognition of better performance when other individuals receive a merit increase of 7 percent.

Another lesson learned, and which is reflected in the new generation of salary increase systems, is that salary increases based on performance should not be commingled with pay increases for other purposes. If, for instance, all employees are to be granted increases of 6 percent for economic reasons, then an employee receiving a performance increase should get at least 13 percent. It is essential that the employee receiving this percentage be told that 6 percent is for economic reasons and 7 percent is for improved performance. It really does not matter too much whether the total increase is granted at one time or in separate amounts at various intervals.

Interestingly enough, many companies, believing that these incentives reward higher productivity and represent investment spending rather than expenses, do not even budget for performance pay increases. The yield from such investment spending is high since there is no capital committed and the investment is made only after the yield is realized. In companies that place no limit on improved performance or greater productivity, there should be no limit on performance pay increases. Furthermore, withholding performance pay increases actually earned by improved effectiveness might become a legitimate grievance from deserving employees.

INCENTIVE PAY PLANS

Several well-proven and highly effective incentive plans for operational employees, particularly those performing repetitive factory jobs, have existed for many years. At the same time however, the number of operational employees covered by these plans has been declining for almost 20 years, as has the percentage of total factory workers receiving these benefits. Apparently, this dramatic declining number of persons can be attributed to basic changes in the nature of production jobs, in which factory jobs are characterized by technical knowledge, worker controlled methods, and operations performed by groups. Such work characteristics make difficult the application of traditionally established factory incentive plans.

Currently, there is some concerted effort by a few leadership companies to modify traditional incentive plans and develop new plans. These modifications attempt to preserve the basic concepts behind incentives and reward individual employees or groups for higher quantity and quality of production by designing plans specifically directed at more technically oriented, diversified positions. It is simply too early to draw any conclusions as to whether or not these efforts will be successful.

But what of financial incentive plans for companies like banks which "produce" only services? In the service industries incentive plans exist only in the executive and professional levels. According to Fortune Magazine incentive plans in the banking industry are designed to attract, retain, and motivate executives. In a study of incentive compensation practices in the Fortune top 50 commercial banking companies, 94% reported either a short term or long term plan in 1979. But these plans which provided well for the management personnel were exclusively in the executive and professional level. In fact, over the past 25 years, incentive compensation plans for executive and professional employees have been developed to a fine art. Originally these incentives were basically profit sharing plans, but as companies developed into multibusiness multiunit organizations, profits of the firm overall, became a poor measuring indicator of the achievement of business unit management.

To meet this problem, goal-oriented programs were introduced about 15 years ago. Essentially, these programs set profit goals at the beginning of each year, or at another measurement period. All participants receive awards based first upon how well the business performs against the present targets, and secondly, upon personal contribution to the overall achievement.

The difficulty with such plans has been the requirement to establish goals before the measurement period begins. The theory is that goals set for each year should represent equivalent management achievement in the light of economic and other circumstances that exist at that time. Such a system has the virtue of providing incentive for management to excel in business units that are essentially less profitable or experiencing difficulties. But, of course, the critical problem is establishing goals before the year begins.

A "new generation" of management incentive compensation plans has evolved during the past few years, attempting to resolve the problem of goal-orientation. Under these plans, the principle quantifiable and qualifiable criteria for measuring managerial performance in each business unit are determined. These criteria may involve such measures as return on investment or turnaround time on inquiries. As few as two and as many as a couple of hundred of criteria have been established. For each of these criteria, rational economic standards and rational production standards are set for target, for minimum, and for maximum achievement. Next, the standards are described and accepted as permanent unless there are basic changes in the business or the economic environment. The numbers themselves may change as conditions change, but the standards remain constant.

The newest development in incentive-pay compensation plans applies to middle-group employees, introducing an entirely new technology. Experience with this designated group has been limited, yet there has been enough evidence to indicate, first, that the plans for these employees can be successfully developed and implemented, and secondly, some principles and guidelines can also be created to enhance these innovative compensation schemes. Three types of plans have evolved and have been applied with success to middle-group employees. These are goal-oriented, discretionary, and special award plans.

GOAL-ORIENTED PLAN

In a goal-oriented plan, the key task is to establish performance criteria. This requires answers to several questions. First, what are the factors that substantially measure performance in the business unit where the incentive plan is being applied? Second, what standards or targets must be established with respect to each of these performance criteria? Third, what system for measuring performance against these standards must be developed? The process of setting targets and standards is extremely difficult. An incentive system for middle-level positions must also provide a system for higher awards for achievement in excess of goals, and lower awards for failure to achieve goals. This is seldom done on a straight formula basis. Finally, plans sometimes provide variations in actual payments for individuals, based on how they contribute to the overall group achievement.

DISCRETIONARY PLAN

Discretionary plans are really the framework for granting some individuals the discretion, and therefore the authority, to pay awards. This includes the discretion or authority to communicate or not to communicate the basis on which awards are made. These plans should obviously not be arbitrary, but inherently they allow considerable latitude to a manager in the application of corporate policy and guidelines. In one such case, Citibank set a budget of three percent of salary to be paid as bonuses to middle-group employees. Each of the departments and units established for administering the plan were advised of this allocation. Corporate staff provided guidelines, policy outlines, requirements, and information to inform and assist managers in developing the specifics of their own incentive programs. Within these very general guidelines, each department then had the authority and responsibility to develop specific performance criteria, the methods of measuring performance, and the system for recognizing individual work contributions.

SPECIAL AWARD PLAN

A third type of incentive plan for middle-group employees is the special award plan. Some of these have been in effect for a long time. The idea of special awards programs is that those who had made extraordinary achievements or accomplishments in their jobs are eligible for awards in the year in which they made the achievements. Typically, under such a program, individual supervisors may recommend any of their people for such an award. There are no limitations in the number of recommendations they may make; the only requirement is that there be genuine achievement. These recommendations are received by higher-level management until they are finally reviewed and approved at top corporate levels. The key to success of special award programs is obviously the definition of what constitutes an extraordinary achievement.

The problem of instituting a financial incentive program in a service industry such as a large bank is illustrated in the fact that a bank is classified as a marginal incentive industry. In 1973, Citibank decided to broaden its incentive program to include all personnel in the corporation. While no study has been done on the results of the program, bank officials feel that production and quality has improved effectively enough to have Citibank challenge Bank of America for the top spot among American banks.

IMPACT ON QUALITY

As in the case of all activities that impact employee quality, it is difficult to establish with any great precision either the actual or potential improvement in quality that results from the adoption of incentive plans. Presently, the types of information systems that make this kind of quantifiable documentation possible for firms do not exist. Still, there are some special studies of incentive plans that give quantitative insights into this problem.

With respect to incentives for operations or production employees, a great number of cases have demonstrated that under the right circumstances, incentive pay plans contribute to greater employee quality. With respect to management incentive compensation plans, there have been two comprehensive studies of business results in bonus and nonbonus paying firms. Both studies concentrated on a comparable group of bonus-paying and nonbonus-paying companies and both showed that by any measure of business success, the bonus-paying firms were more successful than nonbonus-paying companies.

Perhaps the most persuasive evidence of the usefulness of incentive plans in increasing quality are the views of management people in companies that have such plans. Practically all believe that incentives make a positive contribution toward more effective employee work. In fact, it is hard to think of any reason why a company would adopt incentive plans unless it did believe that one of the results would be better productivity and quality.

It is interesting to note that employees themselves generally favor incentive pay plans. Many favor them because they believe that under such plans they will earn more money. This is in the company's interest if the greater money earned reflects higher quality and greater productivity. Many employees also have expressed the view that under an incentive pay plan, the better performers are the better paid employees.

DISINCENTIVES

Contrary to incentives which act as stimuli persuasively compelling employees to change their attitudes and performance for the better, disincentives or deterrents are financial and nonfinancial plans that motivate employees to work less effectively or to do the wrong things. One type of disincentive is the incorrect financial incentive which may motivate people to violate standards, avoid the system, work effectively on the wrong things, or work by the wrong methods. Financial incentive plans that cause negative work attitudes because they are perceived to be unfair or unrealistic, or because they come into conflict with other basic employee values, can be classified as disincentives.

In addition to incorrect financial incentives, there are a variety of other types of disincentives. Promotions based on favoritism or seniority, rather than ability, represents a disincentive to improve performance. Failure to deal with employee questions or grievances in a timely and constructive manner can be a disincentive, too. Similarly, a highly authoritarian style of supervision which creates dissatisfaction among workers is indirectly another kind of disincentive.

Furthermore, particular company action that seems rational may turn out to be a disincentive. For instance, some companies have urged employees to develop better methods of doing the work, with the result that fewer employees were needed. Yet ironically enough, some of those employees who helped work out the better methods were laid off as a consequence. Here, the incentive for better work was to lose one's job which is clearly a disincentive!

Moreover, a salary system that rewards people for something other than the effectiveness of work can be defined as a disincentive since it stimulates people to behave in whatever way the rewards system is geared and will not increase the effectiveness of their work. Pay increases that come automatically with time motivate people to stay in their job in order to get along and survive rather than to work effectively.

Part of the process of building incentives into a company must necessarily be to identify elements of disincentives. A formal personal audit includes identification of disincentives followed by appropriate action plans, which may result in a greater net motivation by removing demotivators. The presence of disincentives may make it difficult to establish positive incentives so that it is advantageous procedurally to identify and remove or neutralize disincentives before steps are taken to adopt or improve positive incentives.

CHAPTER VI

Customer Perception of Quality

"Customers expect more today. We want to get the dope on how we're doing right now, what's actually happening in the trenches." This colorful comment made by AT&T customer services director, Robert Gryb, expresses a keen concern for the customer that is currently being shared by an overwhelming number of service industries. This renewed recognition of the powerful role played by the customer is a result of increased regulation and competition confronting almost all industries today. Consequently, methods to measure a person's interpretation of what he sees, feels, and hears, otherwise referred to as "customer perception," have also received acute attention as instrumental tools for determining customer satisfaction. However, just as no two peoples' perceptions are exactly alike, neither are the techniques used to measure customers' attitudes and beliefs. Rather, there are a variety of techniques available, each having unique characteristics that qualify it for specific research objectives.

MAIL SURVEYS

For instance, mail surveys are conducted among samples of usually hard-to-get respondents with self-administered questionnaires that are shorter than other forms of surveys. The questionnaire is generally mailed with an introductory letter and self-addressed stamped envelope to increase convenience of return. Mail surveys are advantageous because they are usually less expensive than telephone or personal interviewing and do not require a large field staff. The anonymity of mail interviewing allows respondents to be more frank in their answers, especially on sensitive financial issues. Lastly, certain sections of the population may be more easily reached by mail than by other techniques so that a geographically dispersed clientele can be contacted.

On the other hand, sequence bias in which the respondent modifies his individual answers after having read all the questions first, puts a severe limitation on the mail survey. Moreover, mail surveys suffer from a dilemma whereby those who do return their questionnaires tend to be better educated and have greater interest in the topic. And there is never a guarantee that the survey was not filled out by someone other than the intended respondent. Even when these mail questionnaires are returned, they come in so slow and scattered that mail survey completion time is the worst of any technique. Finally, non-response bias proposes the problem of "what about those who didn't return the questionnaire." In view of printing and postage costs and the possible need for follow-up mailing, the cost per return can actually be high if the non-response rate is large.

On the contrary, Chemical Bank has experienced a healthy 25% response rate while utilizing the mail survey method. Questionnaires designed to evaluate the bank's branch services are inserted in customers' monthly statements based on the rationale that "when you open your statement, you're thinking about banking." Mail surveys are sent to half the customers of each of Chemical's 250 branches to identify such problems as unresponsive tellers, lengthy waiting time, and inconvenient hours.

ELECTRONIC SURVEYS

Candid responses have also been gathered by four "pushbutton questionnaires" installed on a rotating basis in each of the one hundred offices of Lloyds Bank California. The instant feedback machines require only thirty seconds of a customer's time to anonymously answer eleven questions including the rating of attention received from branch management, accuracy of servicing accounts, and the courtesy, efficiency, and speed of tellers. The tabulated information is quickly printed out so that management can take immediate action to identify problem areas and improve service. According to executive vice president, Carl Wiese, this pushbutton procedure "shows our customers that we value their opinions and comments enough to provide a quick, easy, private way for them to tell us how we're doing."

Customers are not the only ones questioned about their perceptions of banking services, though. In a "Public Opinion Survey" done at California First Bank, management perceptions as to what the bank's image is to the public is measured by beginning all questions with the inquiry, "How did customers answer the following?" The notion of management employees trying to temporarily fit in the customers' shoes works well to point out any discrepancies between actual customer attitudes and the perceived beliefs employees have as to how their customers view the bank and its services.

PANEL SURVEY

In addition, customer attitudes toward the American Telephone and Telegraph Company are being detected by a questionnaire completed by a panel of 2,200 customers. Begun in 1972, the customer feedback program is called "Public Overview" and is conducted by the National Family Opinion Inc. To properly form the panel, AT&T takes the national census and tries to find 2,200 people who represent roughly the same sort of distribution as in the population at large. The panel is reconstituted every four years, while one quarter of the panel must be replaced every year due to deaths, disappearances, and moving. Panel members are not paid, yet AT&T does give them birthday and Christmas gifts.

Three major attitude indexes are studied—on overall quality of service, overall cost, and company image. Just recently, general questions about the company were tacked on including whether or not AT&T is perceived as a polluter. Curiously enough, panel members have not necessarily had current contact with the phone company so that their opinions are based on such outside factors as rate cases and publicity.

Results clearly indicate that customer attitude toward employees has been deteriorating since the Public Overview Program was initiated. In order to counteract this distressing trend, Bell System managers have worked into their public speeches declarations of AT&T's increasing emphasis on employee courtesy and service.

HANDOUT SURVEYS

One of the most ambitious programs to measure customer perception is the annual "customer service audit" conducted at J.L. Hudson Co., which operates fashion shops and restaurants in Detroit. Initially, a questionnaire touching all aspects of store life is handed out to customers at point of sale. After these forms are mailed back by customers, they are catalogued on a computer and reviewed by a task force composed of top executives in all areas of store management. The task force has a weekly three hour meeting and works like a Senate Investigating Committee examining every facet of operations before brainstorming with a list of recommendations derived from the criticisms contained in the customer audits. To ensure speedy implementations of the task force's suggestions, a point value for service based on the audits is built into each executive's annual performance review. Goals for the improvement of service are built into the company's annual business plans, too.

In order to gain feedback, another merchandise retailing store chain, Zayre, distributes questionnaires printed in five different languages in their "Zayre Cares" pamphlets which outline available customer services such as layaway and exchange plans. In much the same way, at Rich's retail store in Atlanta, question cards are cautiously put in customers' packages and shopping bags. For as vice president for consumer affairs, Ken Rich warns, "We must do this spasmodically. If you do this for very long it becomes old hat to customers and they no longer respond, or their answers are rote. We usually do it for about six to eight weeks at a shot, and get almost 200 responses a week. When interest lags, we discontinue the program."

Not to be excluded, the restaurant industry is also making an ardent effort to gather customer feedback and pinpoint problems by use of the comment card or "table top questionnaire" which is available at tables, counters, and cash registers in a majority of restaurants. Normally, there are no customer incentives to respond to these cards, yet most customers indicate that prepaid postage and easily accessible cards are sufficient reasons to respond. Comment cards have a limited place in the perception research process because customers who voluntarily fill in the cards are not often indicative of the typical guest. Therefore, the question cards are generally best utilized as inner comparison devices for tracking significant operating changes which might accompany a change in management or the menu. Nevertheless, customer comment cards which can either be mailed back, given to an employee, or dropped in a collection box near an exit door, have been frequently used to take definitive follow-up action. Such follow-up action begins with the operations vice president who must analyze and tabulate results from the cards and formulate some conclusions and decisions. A customer card summary is then distributed to top management, regional managers, and unit managers. An unusual example of action taken as a result of analysis of comment cards took place at Win Schuler's restaurant and is reported by Hans Schuler himself.

"A unique onion soup was mentioned on many comment cards as being too thick. The thickness of the soup was considered to be a factor that made the soup a signature item. Instead of changing the recipe, the decision was made to expand the menu description and train the waitress to inform the customer of the consistency of this unique product."

ACTION LINES

Similarly, the First Arizona Bank has developed an Action Line program that uses customer comment forms in all their branch offices in order to measure customer satisfaction. The form's design immediately identifies the nature of the comment; either compliment, suggestion or special problem. It also solicits such detailed information from the customer as purpose of the visit to the bank, services used, and waiting time for service. When collected and reviewed in volume, this data reveals problem areas experienced by different branches.

TELEPHONE SURVEYS

Customer attitudinal measurement can also be accurately measured by the telephone interview. Telephone calls are made to a random sample of clients in designated geographic areas with each call lasting about 10 to 15 minutes. An appealing aspect of the telephone interview is that a high number of respondents can be obtained with a minimum of effort, making it an extremely economical and efficient technique. Quality Control can be kept at a near perfect level since interviews are conducted from one centralized location and a field supervisor is able to listen in on any interview to assure it is being correctly conducted. Quality Control can further be enhanced by employing a professional interviewing staff and using the WATS lines to call into any area of the country. And once the calls are put through, 80 to 90% of the customers contacted will agree to complete the interview. As with mail surveys, people are more likely to answer candidly because of the element of anonymity.

Unfortunately, the telephone interview cannot be as long as in-home interviews, and people who do not have telephones are excluded, permitting a chance for bias. However, it should be noted that only 5% of American households are phoneless, and probably such individuals would not be financial institution customers anyway.

With only 5% of American households without a phone, AT&T has become "The Biggest Company on Earth" and has developed TELSAM (telephone service attitude measurement), a customer feedback project that conducts one million telephone interviews annually in order to round up opinion from its 55 million customers. Female homemakers do most of the day interviewing and college students work there at night with as many as 45 employees asking customers about their latest encounters with the Bell System at any one time. Normally, an interviewer will ask the customer to rate the promptness of an operator or give the degree of courtesy shown by a repairman. All this critical information is collected at a TELSAM site in either Pennsylvania or Denver, each being run by separate research firms. After that, all the customer data is pumped into a central computer from which monthly reports are made and sent to the Bell System management for review and possible action. Demonstrably, it was discovered through the TELSAM project that customers favored a more personalized telephone approach in which operators answer with their own names when they pick up a call. Immediately, operators adopted the new personalized procedure in order to heighten customer satisfaction.

INTERVIEWS

The financial service arena has also tuned into the telephone interview as a vital vehicle for discovering customer perception. "The Middle Market Banking Study" done by an outside marketing service for Mellon Bank, relied upon the flexible telephone technique to question 500 financial executives of randomly selected firms in the Pittsburgh area which have annual sales between $3 and $50 million. Questions asked during the interview were based solely on primary commercial banking relationships and covered such areas as degree of satisfaction with primary banks, factors considered most important in the choice of a commercial banking institution, and rating of primary banks in terms of these key factors. Respondents' responses were geographically grouped into both Pittsburgh's county market and suburban market for tabulation. Data was presented for the total sample in terms of industry groups (e.g., manufacturing, wholesale trade, etc.) and sales volume ranges. Where appropriate, recap tables were provided to facilitate review.

In addition to the mail and telephone interviews, customer perception can be measured by the personal interview. Respondents are randomly selected for interviews either in their homes or offices so that the interviewer must secure in advance the respondent's permission to participate in the interview. This type of interview can generally be more lengthy because there are less pressures on the part of the respondent to terminate, if the respondent has already invited the interviewer into his home or office. In such a face-to-face situation, the interviewer has the ability to probe more effectively and incorporate any body language into the respondent's comments, adding another measure of quality in those areas of questioning where it is applicable. When visual support for the perceptions being researched is helpful or necessary, the interviewer can show the respondent samples of the product and easily use data collection devices such as rating scales and card sorting techniques.

On the negative side, the personal interview is one of the most costly techniques because of travel expenses and the high number of visits that are needed. Sampling bias is becoming harder to control since some interviewers refuse to conduct in-home interviews in transition neighborhoods. Such communities however, still contain many senior citizens who may not have high assets but concentrate what they have in savings deposits and thus, are of some importance to bankers. Worse yet, the face-to-face element of the personal interview can intimidate the respondent and prevent candid participation. And because supervisors are unable to overhear the actual face-to-face interview being conducted, they are less able to be aware of the interviewers' effectiveness in dealing with the respondent.

Fortunately, Greenwich Research Associates have overcome the problems plaguing the personal interview and have effectively employed this method to discover current perceptions in large corporate banking. This survey's sample is based primarily on corporations listed in the Fortune Double 500 Directory and supplemented by lists of leading U.S. corporations published in other business magazines. The total universe includes 1,861 of the nation's largest corporations of which 1,140 are chosen to complete the interviews, representing all large corporations' sales rank and industry groups.

Care is taken to interview only corporate executives having direct responsibility for banking decisions. An initial request for an interview is directed to the vice president of finance or to the treasurer. Each executive then receives a letter of introduction and explanation of the survey. These executives are encouraged to include their assistants in the interview or in a separately conducted one, as they tend to be specialists in day-to-day bank relations, cash management and operations. Next, each executive is telephoned for an appointment at the time and place of his choice. Afterwards, a letter confirming the appointment is sent out with an enclosed worksheet dealing with questions on domestic borrowings, cash balances, non-credit services, etc. The worksheet, by covering dollar volume and "use" tables, increases response accuracy, eases the work of the executive in accumulating information, and shortens the personal interview time.

These personal interviews, conducted by trained businessmen, cover a company's dealings with its banks and its overall banking policies to evaluate the strengths and weaknesses of each bank as seen by its large corporate customers. Every major bank in every region of the country is evaluated. To accomplish this, each executive is shown a list of 70 banks and is asked a series of questions concerning solicitations for each bank. Secondly, all executives are asked to list on a self-administered form, the banks they use most for domestic and international banking.

The questionnaire for this large-scale research has six different versions to expand the scope of the research. Each company's financial officer is asked to evaluate his bank's calling officers, top management, credit and pricing policies, operational capabilities, and service usage. At the onset of the interview, the respondent is given a Card Deck with labeled cards he is asked to refer to for certain questions. These cards contain descriptive lists of banking services, banking advantages, etc., which are individually coded so that a respondent's verbal answer can be easily tabulated by the interviewer on a corresponding form.

After completion of the over one thousand interviews, data is compiled by Greenwich Research in an annual report sold to banking institutions throughout the country. Specific reports included in this research, such as the Competitive Situation Report, the Penetration Report, and the Special Action Report, are used by various divisions of banks to identify trends and improve services. Examples of several of Greenwich's reports are included at the end of the chapter.

The personal interview technique was also chosen by The Bank Research Associates in their attempt to accurately measure banking customers' perceptions of automated services and bank machines. With this method, sophisticated scaler techniques could be utilized in 300 randomly selected in-home interviews conducted during 1976 in a large midwestern metropolitan city. Data collection tools for the interviews consisted of demographic questions relating to age, income and the like; open-ended questions on bank machines, and stimuli statements on individual cards relating to specific attributes of banking machines.

Q-SORTS

To clarify this unique "Q-sort" methodology, the respondent was given a deck of 29 cards containing a single statement on each card and was asked to make comparative preferences by sorting the cards along a six-point scale ranging from strongly disagree (1) to strongly agree (6). The scale was printed on a board placed before the respondent (without numerical values) and contained an even number of positions to force a determination of whether or not there was agreement or disagreement with the statement. The stimulus for the sort was: "In My Opinion A Bank Machine Should." Statements following this stimulus included; "give me a printed statement describing my transactions; be found in all major grocery stores; and, be the way most banking will be done in the future."

The data generated from the Q-sort technique allowed an analysis by statements through rankings of percentages and intensity of agreement. A frequency distribution was constructed for each statement for the "agree" side (4, 5, or 6), each slot was totaled, and means and percentages were computed and ranked. Similar statistics were developed for the "disagree" side. To furnish insight into the intensity of the respondents' feelings, an agree potency index (API) was created and then ranked so that the perceptual intensity of the various statements could be determined. This empirical investigation is still being continued on an ongoing basis to identify and monitor changes in the consumer's perceptions of banking services.

SEMANTIC DIFFERENTIAL

Another scaler technique that is commonly called upon for personal interviews and even mail surveys, is the semantic differential. The semantic differential measures the meaning that a concept might have for individuals by using three major scales or dimensions. Namely, the evaluative scales which measure favorable and unfavorable dimensions, the potency scales which measure strong and weak dimensions, and the activity scales which measure fast and slow dimensions. The subject is asked to rate the concept (institution) on a series of seven- or five-point scales. These scales are bipolar in that the end points on the scale represent extreme opposite opinions. An example would be:

Pleasant Employees ⟸⟹ Unpleasant Employees

When incorporating the semantic differential into a research study there are basically two separate groups who can act as subjects. First, the study can utilize only non-customers (potential customers) of each institution to perform the ratings. If non-customers are utilized, the scales should be constructed in a balance format. That is, an even number of both favorable and unfavorable points around a center or neutral point of each dimension.

The second option available is using only present customers of each bank to rate their own bank. Because a customer of a bank will often tend to see only the favorable aspects of his bank and suppress the negative views he may have, an unbalanced scale should be used with a larger number of points on the scale at the positive side. An unbalanced scale where there are four favorable, one neutral, and two unfavorable points eliminates "end piling" at a single point on the scale. If both customers' and non-customers' perceptions are obtained for a single institution, they should be presented as separate graphic profiles.

Both the Q-sort and the semantic differential are important research tools for intercept interviewing. Here, individuals are selected at random to be interviewed on location at shopping centers, coming out of offices or at other public areas where a fairly typical cross section of the prime audience sought can be found. The participants are approached by an interviewer who asks their cooperation by answering a few questions. The moderator then takes the participant to a nearby location away from the mainstream of traffic to conduct a structured interview using a pre-approved questionnaire. Because of a high number of people located in the area, a number of interviews can be readily obtained within a short period of time, which controls interview expense. Better yet, the homogeneity of the participants can be automatically controlled by the selection of the site. Most assuredly then, if an organization wants to interview its customers on some particular aspect of service, intercepting them as they leave the bank building would give a 100% homogeneous group of customers.

At the other end of the spectrum is the fact that most of the participants are in a hurry and will not tolerate lengthy discussions. And in some cases, such as outside an office, it becomes apparent who the interviewing is being done for and the anonymity of the sponsoring firm is lost. Or the respondent, if aware of the sponsor, may be inclined to respond more positively towards the participating sponsor while on his home ground.

FOCUS GROUPS

This "home ground" bias is eliminated with the focus group interview, another research tool conducted on "neutral ground" in the office of a professional research service. Focus groups usually range in size from eight to 12 individuals who are assembled together with a qualified group leader for discussion of some specific aspect of banking. The group interview sessions can last from an hour to two hours with participants being selected by the research service using current demographic data. The primary role of the moderator is to encourage a good give-and-take among participants about the subject at hand, making sure that no one individual controls the group discussion. At the end of the session a detailed written report is drawn up by the leader and submitted to the financial institution.

The interaction of group members can be particularly beneficial because it tends to relax each respondent, providing a better source of information than in a one-on-one situation. The more natural environment brings out peoples' views, thoughts, and positive and negative feelings toward the subject. The profile of these participants can be tightly structured so that the group can be all females, all people who are heavy users of charge cards, etc. This homogeneous group composition provides an opportunity to gain attitudes of a very specific, prime prospect kind of consumer within the marketplace. Body language and voice inflection expressed in the focus discussions add an extra dimension for interpretation of respondents' comments by the moderator and even by the client when sessions are videotaped. Focus group interviews are especially useful for gathering information and input on major issues that can later be incorporated into a questionnaire for a quantitative study.

Quantitative research is not provided by focus discussions—only qualitative data can be extracted because with such a small sample the reactions of participants in the group cannot be projected to the entire marketplace. It can also be difficult to assemble special interest groups, particularly professionals with demanding schedules.

Nonetheless, this focus group approach has become a major adjunct to the research efforts at The Farmers and Mechanics Savings Bank in Minneapolis. There, participants are paid a mere $5, making the total cost $300 per session including the final report submitted by the moderator. Given the meager payment, motivation for the participants seems to be the opportunity to influence the bank and be made to feel important.

Introduction of a "Bank by Phone" service, the first such program of its kind in the country, and a project particularly important in a unit banking state like Minnesota, only successfully emerged after focus group discussions in which participants explained that the preliminary version was too complicated and would not be understood by the average bank customer. Further refinements were made and currently, the only "problem" with the Bank by Phone service is its overwhelming popularity!

Ralph Klapperich, F and M's marketing vice president, who is able to observe session responses firsthand through a two-way mirror, insists the focus interview has features that no other research method can offer. "It is a two-way communication and because it is unstructured and somewhat open-ended, it is a device for getting closer to your customers, which can only benefit both the institution and the public," he says.

Win Barnes, vice president of Shell Motorist Club couldn't agree more with Mr. Klapperich. Barnes, who is also manager of the direct mail division for Shell Oil Company, sees the focus group interview as a diagnostic tool that "is not for the timid. These people tell you exactly how they feel." Consequently, through a series of focus discussions held in three major cities across the country, Shell learned that their customers did not rank the Club's benefits in the same order of importance that the Shell management thought they would. Ironically enough, some of the benefits Shell executives thought to be most important turned out to be least important and vice-versa!

A more aggressive stance on customer input has also been adopted by a Minneapolis retail store called Dayton's. At Dayton's, focus interviews are conducted under the guise of "consumer advisory panels." The panel consists of twenty customers selected randomly from charge account lists or recommended by former panel members. A monthly luncheon is held at which a different consumer topic is discussed each time. Panel members may be asked to shop in a specified department and then compare with other stores, or asked their opinions on advertisements. Store manager, Reuel Nygoard, admits suggestions from the panel have resulted in the addition of a swim shop along with other changes in customer service.

In a far-fetched fashion, employee meetings may be considered as a vehicle for focus discussions and a chance to learn about customers' perceptions. In the opinion of Unicare Food Services' President, Ed Lump, he states, "Sometimes the best way to find out how customers feel is to probe employees in a general meeting or private conference; at times customers will say things to them they will not say to management."

SHOPPER SURVEYS

Unknowingly, employees can provide further insights into customer perception through shopper surveys that enable specific customer service to be audited by an outside agency. In a shopper survey, trained surveyors pose as inquiring or transacting customers to evaluate employees on "customer contact performance."

Primary Customer Perception Research Techniques

Techniques	Description	Benefits
Mail Survey	• Self-administered questionnaire • Shorter than other survey forms • Mail with self-addressed, stamped envelope	1. Anonymity allows candid response 2. Reaches geographically dispersed clientele 3. Small field staff required
Comment Cards	• "Table top questionnaire" available at tables, counters, etc. • Cards are either mailed back, given to an employee or dropped in collection box • Identifies compliment, complaint, or suggestion	1. Solicits information for follow-up action to improve services 2. Inner comparison device to track operating changes which accompany change in management
Telephone Interview	• Random sample of customers in designed geographic area • Phone call lasts 10-15 minutes	1. Efficient—obtain high number of respondents with minimum effort 2. Superior Quality Control 3. 80-90% response rate 4. Anonymity allows candid responses
Hotline	• Direct communication link between customer and company • Provides personal contact so that customers can resolve complaints and questions • Firm can solicit advice on service attributes	1. Turn irritated customer into source of perception information 2. Can provide personal source of information for customers
Personal Interview	• Respondents randomly selected for interviews in their homes or offices • Face to face situation • Interviewer must secure in advance participants permission	1. Interviews can be lengthy 2. Interviewer can probe more effectively 3. Body language can be incorporated as another measure of quality 4. Visual supports can be used
Intercept Interview	• Respondents randomly approached on location at shopping center, bank, etc. • Interviewer takes participants to nearby quieter location • Conducts interview with pre-approved questionnaire	1. Able to control homogeneity of participants by site selected 2. Many interviews can be conducted in short time 3. Visual supports can be used
Focus Group Interview	• 3 to 12 individuals discuss specific issue with qualified moderator • Sessions last from 1-2 hours • At end of session moderator draws up written report	1. Interaction of members relaxes respondents in more natural environment 2. Profile of participants can be tightly structured 3. Body language adds measure of quality 4. Visual and graphic presentations can be made
Shopper Survey	• Trained surveyors pose as inquiring or transacting bank customers • Surveyors evaluate employees on "customer contact performance" • Banks participate in survey together	1. Provides uniform, measurable standards of performance for customer contact people 2. Provides comparative data for all participating banks 3. Identifies areas of strengths and weaknesses, so that banks can take corrective action
Complaint Bureau	• Includes acknowledgement of complaints, assignment of responsibility for handling complaints, and close-out of complaints • Computerized system controls, tracks, and analyzes customer complaints • Handles mailed, telephoned, and personal complaints	1. Identifies trends and problem areas 2. Convinces customer of company's desire to be responsive to their problems
Feedback Machine	• "Pushbutton questionnaire" that requires only 30 seconds to anonymously answer questions and rate services • Tabulated information quickly printed out	1. Identifies problem areas immediately 2. Easy, private method 3. Shows customers that sponsoring firm values their options

Limitations	Relative Cost	Relative Turnaround Time	Relative Staff Resource
1. Strong non-response bias 2. Response bias 3. Sequence bias 4. Slowest completion time	Inexpensive	Slow	Small
1. Strong response bias 2. Noncustomer response bias	Inexpensive	Medium	Small
1. Interview does not last long 2. Can't use graphic samples 3. Phoneless households are excluded	Expensive	Prompt	Large
1. Strong response bias	Expensive	Prompt	Large
1. Hinders candid participation 2. Direct supervisory control of interviewers difficult 3. Sampling bias—transition neighborhoods may be avoided	Expensive	Slow	Large
1. Respondents won't tolerate lengthy discussions 2. Anonymity of sponsoring firm may be lost 3. Homeground bias makes participants respond more positively than usual	Moderate	Medium	Medium
1. Only provides qualitative data 2. It's difficult to assemble special interest groups—e.g., professionals with demanding schedules 3. Problem of "no-show"	Moderate	Prompt	Medium
1. Shopper exposure high so that surveyors may be identified by bank personnel	Expensive	Slow	Large
1. If complaints are shunted to low-level personnel, customer mistrust and hostility develops 2. Difficult to keep track of daily routes taken by each complaint	Expensive	Prompt	Large
1. Can't obtain qualitative responses 2. Some customers may be afraid to use the machine	Moderate	Prompt	Small

These shoppers measure, in the case of the banking business, the customer contact performance of tellers, receptionists, and new accounts personnel on the basis of their work performance, their customer relations skills, product knowledge, cross-sales efforts, and closing comments. Once field work is completed, the questionnaires listing all rating criteria mentioned above are edited and turned over for data processing. Two types of ratings are applied to measure customer contact performance. The first is a percentage of positive answers to specific points being shopped. An example would be: "Was there a line?" The second type of measurement asks shoppers to evaluate performance on a five-point rating scale, where one is the highest rating. This scaling technique measures attitudinal differences that could not be handled by an absolute "yes-no" answer. A typical case would be receptionist measurement for helpfulness with the overall response being a 1.94 on a 3.0 scale.

The final report is based on the computer printouts and illustrates performance findings with table charts. Uniform, measurable standards of performance for customer contact people are established. Such a summary of results pinpoints areas of strengths and weaknesses so that corrective actions can be taken. As with the "Chicago Loop Shopping Survey," many banks participate in a shopper survey together, not only to gain input about the performance of their own customer contact people, but to also obtain the merged performance data of other banks for comparison purposes.

INQUIRIES AND COMPLAINTS

Inquiries, complaints and comparisons are crucial because thanks in part to consumerism, customers are demanding much more today. Consequently, close attention must be given to customer complaints and inquiries which have become so highly sophisticated that the enlightened airlines industry no longer views complaints as negative problems but rather, "suggestions in disguise." No matter the viewpoint, registered complaints sound out customers' perceptions only too loud and clear.

That's why the essential features of any complaint handling program should include: prompt acknowledgement of complaints, clear assignment of responsibility for handling and investigating the complaint, and prompt close-out of the complaint with a two-week target where practicable. The major goal of such a program is to convince customers of the company's genuine concern and desire to be responsive to any problems they may encounter.

At Manufacturers Hanover Trust, a computerized customer inquiry reporting system controls, tracks, and analyzes communications received by respondent, corporate, and brokerage customers. The most significant aspect of the new system is that it distinguishes between controllable and non-controllable branch and consumer credit incidents. Attitude, efficiency or performance-related problems are controllable ones which bank personnel can correct. The non-controllable incidents are those outside the direct control of branch personnel like central bookkeeping and data processing.

Wells Fargo Bank in California has also computerized their procedures for complaint-handling. All written complaints are routed through a Customer Relations Center. Then when it receives a complaint, the center simultaneously enters it into the computer and forwards it to the administrative office of the department in question. The center allows the department two days to acknowledge to the customer receipt of the complaint, and then 10 days to solve the problem or to notify the customers that progress is being made. Meanwhile, progress toward resolution is updated daily on the computer system. Data on complaint correspondence is maintained by an extensive system of codes identifying the source and type of correspondence, its status, and each action taken.

Once the complaint has been resolved and a solution has been communicated to the customer, the responding department forwards a copy of its response to the center, which checks to make sure that a solution really was found and tries to determine whether some changes in bank policies are warranted.

The center prepares quarterly reports on the complaints received, broken down by the product or service involved. For senior management, the center also prepares year-to-date summaries that highlight trends to identify particular problem areas.

HOT LINES

The "hotline" is yet another recent tool which a number of firms have instituted to facilitate communications, which of course, includes the registering of complaints. A hotline provides a direct two-way communication link whereby a company can gauge the customer's overall impression of the firm or solicit advice on service attributes.

What's more, the First National Bank of Oregon is turning its own hotline, known as the "Savers' Hotline" into a source of personal information for its customers. The Savers' Hotline was initiated in the summer of 1979 to help consumers understand changes in the regular savings rate and in time deposit requirements, which were authorized by the Federal Reserve Board. It was available to all Oregonians, free of charge, from June 23 to August 3, from 7 a.m. to 7 p.m., seven days a week.

During the six weeks the Hotline was in operation, approximately 750 calls were received, with Mondays tending to be busiest. Interestingly enough, about one quarter of the calls came from branch personnel who were unable to sufficiently answer branch customers' questions. The Hotline staff was made up of management trainees.

Since it was the first time the $3.4 billion deposit bank which is Oregon's largest and oldest bank, ever tried anything like the Hotline, they admit, "We weren't fully aware of what type of response we would get. But it was less than we had reasonably anticipated ... we would have been more pleased with a higher response but the Hotline was introduced as a trial—strictly on a test basis."

Even with the low response rate the personal source of information provided by the Hotline was appreciated by a number of people. According to Paul Haist, manager of the bank's Public Relations department, "Most people expected to hear a recording and were grateful to speak with a live, breathing person."

Other industries such as Shell Oil Company and Zayre have integrated well-advertised toll free 800 hotlines into their operations so that customers may call in complaints or just inquire about something. Corrective action programs at Whirlpool and Chrysler have established hotlines to help customers reach responsible company officials with their inquiries or complaints. Otherwise, if customer complaints are ignored or shunted to low-level personnel who are neither trained nor measured on their response to angry complainants, consumer mistrust and outright hostility can be created.

Admittedly, the hotline is an expensive addition to the service program, but most companies that have them regard them as good investments, especially if they can turn irritated customers into sources of perception information.

And perception information from the customer is exactly what interviews, focus groups, surveys, comment cards, complaint bureaus, and hotlines are trying to capture. Granted, there is no one technique that is most appropriate for every research project, yet it appears that the mail survey is the most popular method utilized to gain customer feedback. Very simply, it is an easy and inexpensive procedure. The most efficient research tool is the telephone interview. This flexible method does not succumb to the notoriously poor response rate characteristic of the mail survey. More importantly, the quality control that can be maintained with the telephone interview is superior.

Still, these two techniques are not without their weaknesses. Both rely solely on quantitative data, ignoring any qualitative measure derived from body language or visual supports. The personal interview, however, is able to extract more in-depth information. At the same time, it should be noted that while the personal interview may include the added dimension of body language, it also involves a face-to-face encounter that tends to suppress candid responses.

In today's marketplace though, candid responses are rarely discouraged as the 1980's consumer voices his positive and negative opinions at full volume. Such an up-front and demanding character currently assumed by customers has forced companies to take more expedient or even immediate corrective actions to improve their products and services. In this never-ending attempt to improve services no one follow-up trend stands out except the factor of timeliness as managements strive to fulfill customers' desires and needs.

CHAPTER VII

Sample Surveys and Perception Results

Seven Sample Survey questions and formats follow. Sample Surveys 1 through 3 are examples of surveys to determine an individual financial institutions specific rating for individual attributes.

The format used can be instrumental in determining which service attributes are important. Once the very and extremely important are determined then additional, periodic surveys should be conducted to determine on a scale how well the financial institution is performing.

These customer perceptions can be used to set standards and provide emphasis for performance improvement.

Sample Surveys 5 and 6 are examples of surveys to compare two or more financial institutions and how their attributes compare. Those that customers see as less important (as indicated in Sample Surveys 1-3) need not concern your institution. Those that are important in the customer's perception that are rated lower than the competition indicate tougher standards and improvement actions.

Sample Surveys 6 and 7 indicate how well your financial institution is meeting customer perceptions (standards). Only important attributes should be explored on this survey instrument.

Survey Results examples are shown in Survey Results 1 through 4. Demonstrated are several methods to report customer perceptions of attributes courtesy of Greenwich Research Associates.

Customer perception surveys or feedback complete the Quality Management System and make the final link for setting quality standards and motivating employees.

QUALITY CONTROL SYSTEM

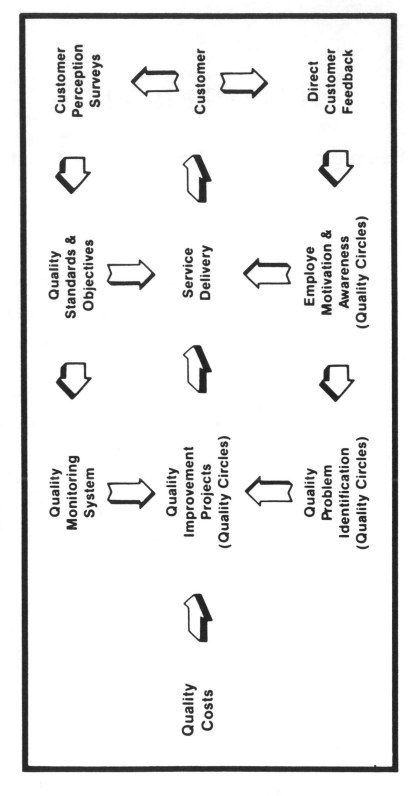

Sample Survey 1 (Determining Attributes)

In dealing with a Financial Institution, how important to you is each of the *service characteristics* listed below?

	Extremely Important	Very Important	Somewhat Important	Not Important
Offers fast service	☐	☐	☐	☐
Offers a variety of financial services	☐	☐	☐	☐
Offers personalized service	☐	☐	☐	☐
Does a good job of handling transactions by mail	☐	☐	☐	☐
Provides error-free or nearly error-free service	☐	☐	☐	☐
Does a good job of coordinating the different types of accounts a customer has	☐	☐	☐	☐
Offers friendly, courteous service	☐	☐	☐	☐
Does a good job of handling transactions by phone	☐	☐	☐	☐

Sample Survey 2 (Determining Attributes)

(Please continue describing how important each attribute is to you)

A Financial Institution that is	Not Important	Somewhat Important	Very Important	Extremely Important
Pacemakers	☐ 1	☐ 2	☐ 3	☐ 4
Warm.	☐ 1	☐ 2	☐ 3	☐ 4
Human	☐ 1	☐ 2	☐ 3	☐ 4
Hard working	☐ 1	☐ 2	☐ 3	☐ 4
Big	☐ 1	☐ 2	☐ 3	☐ 4
International	☐ 1	☐ 2	☐ 3	☐ 4
Opportunistic	☐ 1	☐ 2	☐ 3	☐ 4
Solid	☐ 1	☐ 2	☐ 3	☐ 4
Eastern	☐ 1	☐ 2	☐ 3	☐ 4
Authoritative	☐ 1	☐ 2	☐ 3	☐ 4
Creative.	☐ 1	☐ 2	☐ 3	☐ 4
Futuristic	☐ 1	☐ 2	☐ 3	☐ 4
Ambitious.	☐ 1	☐ 2	☐ 3	☐ 4
Empathetic	☐ 1	☐ 2	☐ 3	☐ 4
Honest	☐ 1	☐ 2	☐ 3	☐ 4
Perceptive.	☐ 1	☐ 2	☐ 3	☐ 4
Inventive	☐ 1	☐ 2	☐ 3	☐ 4
Lofty	☐ 1	☐ 2	☐ 3	☐ 4
Professional	☐ 1	☐ 2	☐ 3	☐ 4
Venerable	☐ 1	☐ 2	☐ 3	☐ 4
Sharp.	☐ 1	☐ 2	☐ 3	☐ 4
Try harder	☐ 1	☐ 2	☐ 3	☐ 4
Accessible.	☐ 1	☐ 2	☐ 3	☐ 4
Forthright.	☐ 1	☐ 2	☐ 3	☐ 4
Aware	☐ 1	☐ 2	☐ 3	☐ 4
Democratic	☐ 1	☐ 2	☐ 3	☐ 4
Selective	☐ 1	☐ 2	☐ 3	☐ 4
Stodgy	☐ 1	☐ 2	☐ 3	☐ 4
Aggressive	☐ 1	☐ 2	☐ 3	☐ 4
Exciting.	☐ 1	☐ 2	☐ 3	☐ 4
Broadminded	☐ 1	☐ 2	☐ 3	☐ 4
Intellectual	☐ 1	☐ 2	☐ 3	☐ 4
Influential.	☐ 1	☐ 2	☐ 3	☐ 4
Clubbish	☐ 1	☐ 2	☐ 3	☐ 4
Conservative.	☐ 1	☐ 2	☐ 3	☐ 4

Sample Survey 3 (Determining Attributes)

(Please continue describing how important each attribute is to you)

A Financial Institution that is	Not Important	Somewhat Important	Very Important	Extremely Important
Progressive	☐ 1	☐ 2	☐ 3	☐ 4
Reliable	☐ 1	☐ 2	☐ 3	☐ 4
Approachable	☐ 1	☐ 2	☐ 3	☐ 4
Specialists	☐ 1	☐ 2	☐ 3	☐ 4
Boastful	☐ 1	☐ 2	☐ 3	☐ 4
Austere	☐ 1	☐ 2	☐ 3	☐ 4
Forward looking	☐ 1	☐ 2	☐ 3	☐ 4
Flexible	☐ 1	☐ 2	☐ 3	
Knowledgeable	☐ 1	☐ 2	☐ 3	☐ 4
Isolated	☐ 1	☐ 2	☐ 3	☐ 4
Prestigious	☐ 1	☐ 2	☐ 3	☐ 4
Technically advanced	☐ 1	☐ 2	☐ 3	☐ 4
Responsive	☐ 1	☐ 2	☐ 3	☐ 4
Unique	☐ 1	☐ 2	☐ 3	☐ 4
Pros	☐ 1	☐ 2	☐ 3	☐ 4
Modern	☐ 1	☐ 2	☐ 3	☐ 4
Outgoing	☐ 1	☐ 2	☐ 3	☐ 4
Bullish	☐ 1	☐ 2	☐ 3	☐ 4
Friendly	☐ 1	☐ 2	☐ 3	☐ 4
Unlimited	☐ 1	☐ 2	☐ 3	
Snobbish	☐ 1	☐ 2	☐ 3	☐ 4
Old-fashioned	☐ 1	☐ 2	☐ 3	☐ 4
Formidable	☐ 1	☐ 2	☐ 3	☐ 4
Sexy	☐ 1	☐ 2	☐ 3	☐ 4
Attentive	☐ 1	☐ 2	☐ 3	☐ 4
Impersonal	☐ 1	☐ 2	☐ 3	☐ 4
Bureaucratic	☐ 1	☐ 2	☐ 3	☐ 4
Grass roots	☐ 1	☐ 2	☐ 3	☐ 4
Action making	☐ 1	☐ 2	☐ 3	☐ 4
Scientific	☐ 1	☐ 2	☐ 3	☐ 4
Dominating	☐ 1	☐ 2	☐ 3	☐ 4
Insular	☐ 1	☐ 2	☐ 3	☐ 4
Resourceful	☐ 1	☐ 2	☐ 3	☐ 4
Traditional	☐ 1	☐ 2	☐ 3	☐ 4

Sample Survey 4 (Comparing Institutions)

In this part of the questionnaire we are interested in your attitudes toward different financial institutions.

For each of the listings below, such as "for fast service," indicate which you think are generally better by checking the box under bank.

	Financial Institution A	Financial Institution B
For fast service	☐	☐
For mortgage loans	☐	☐
For personalized service	☐	☐
For error-free service	☐	☐
For a regular savings account	☐	☐
For meeting all my credit needs	☐	☐
For friendly, courteous service	☐	☐
For providing a variety of financial services	☐	☐
For a savings certificate (time deposit)	☐	☐
For handling transactions by mail	☐	☐
For handling transactions by phone	☐	☐

Sample Survey 5 (Comparing Institutions)

For each of the listings below, such as "for fast service," indicate which Financial Institution you *think* is best by writing "1" in the space under the appropriate institution. Then indicate which you *think* is second best by writing "2" under that Institution. (We're interested in your opnions of these institutions, regardless of whether or not you use them.)

	Financial Institution A	Financial Institution B	Financial Institution C	Financial Institution D
For fast service	_____	_____	_____	_____
For mortgage loans	_____	_____	_____	_____
For checking account	_____	_____	_____	_____
For other checking account services such as overdraft protection and automatic banking cards	_____	_____	_____	_____
For financial counseling in general	___	___		
For personalized service	_____	_____	_____	_____
For trust services	_____	_____	_____	_____
For error-free service	_____	_____	_____	_____
For a regular savings account	_____	_____	_____	_____
For personal loans	_____	_____	_____	_____
For friendly, courteous service	_____	_____	_____	_____
For investment advice for stocks		___		
For investment advice for bonds	_____	_____	_____	_____
For providing a variety of financial services	_____	_____	_____	_____
For a savings certificate (time deposit)	_____	_____	_____	_____
For handling transactions by mail	_____	_____	_____	_____
For coordinating the different types of accounts a customer has	_____	_____	_____	_____
For handling transactions by phone	_____	_____	_____	_____
For meeting the special financial service needs of executives and professionals	_____	_____	_____	_____
For highly specialized financial services in areas such as real estate, commodity trading and international banking	_____	_____	_____	_____
For money market instruments	_____	_____	_____	_____
Best overall for your own banking needs	_____	_____	_____	_____

Sample Survey 6 (Attribute Conformance)

Name of the Financial Institution Your Bank	Describes The Bank Perfectly	Very Well	Fairly Well	Slightly	Doesn't Describe It At All
Pacemakers	☐ 1	☐ 2	☐ 3	☐ 4	☐ 5
Warm.	☐ 1	☐ 2	☐ 3	☐ 4	☐ 5
Human	☐ 1	☐ 2	☐ 3	☐ 4	☐ 5
Hard working	☐ 1	☐ 2	☐ 3	☐ 4	
Big	☐ 1	☐ 2	☐ 3	☐ 4	☐ 5
International	☐ 1	☐ 2	☐ 3	☐ 4	☐ 5
Opportunistic	☐ 1	☐ 2	☐ 3	☐ 4	☐ 5
Solid	☐ 1	☐ 2	☐ 3	☐ 4	☐ 5
Eastern	☐ 1	☐ 2	☐ 3	☐ 4	☐ 5
Authoritative	☐ 1	☐ 2	☐ 3	☐ 4	☐ 5
Creative.	☐ 1	☐ 2	☐ 3	☐ 4	☐ 5
Futuristic	☐ 1	☐ 2	☐ 3	☐ 4	☐ 5
Ambitious.	☐ 1	☐ 2	☐ 3	☐ 4	☐ 5
Empathetic	☐ 1	☐ 2	☐ 3	☐ 4	☐ 5
Honest	☐ 1	☐ 2	☐ 3	☐ 4	☐ 5
Perceptive.	☐ 1	☐ 2	☐ 3	☐ 4	☐ 5
Inventive	☐ 1	☐ 2	☐ 3	☐ 4	☐ 5
Lofty	☐ 1	☐ 2	☐ 3	☐ 4	☐ 5
Professional	☐ 1	☐ 2	☐ 3	☐ 4	☐ 5
Venerable.	☐ 1	☐ 2	☐ 3	☐ 4	☐ 5
Autocratic.	☐ 1	☐ 2	☐ 3	☐ 4	☐ 5
Sharp.	☐ 1	☐ 2	☐ 3	☐ 4	☐ 5
Try harder	☐ 1	☐ 2	☐ 3	☐ 4	☐ 5
Accessible.	☐ 1	☐ 2	☐ 3	☐ 4	☐ 5
Forthright.	☐ 1	☐ 2	☐ 3	☐ 4	☐ 5
Aware	☐ 1	☐ 2	☐ 3	☐ 4	☐ 5
Democratic	☐ 1	☐ 2	☐ 3	☐ 4	☐ 5
Selective	☐ 1	☐ 2	☐ 3	☐ 4	☐ 5
Stodgy	☐ 1	☐ 2	☐ 3	☐ 4	☐ 5
Aggressive	☐ 1	☐ 2	☐ 3	☐ 4	☐ 5
Exciting.	☐ 1	☐ 2	☐ 3	☐ 4	☐ 5
Broadminded	☐ 1	☐ 2	☐ 3	☐ 4	☐ 5
Intellectual	☐ 1	☐ 2	☐ 3	☐ 4	☐ 5
Influential.	☐ 1	☐ 2	☐ 3	☐ 4	☐ 5
Clubbish	☐ 1	☐ 2	☐ 3	☐ 4	☐ 5
Conservative.	☐ 1	☐ 2	☐ 3	☐ 4	☐ 5

Sample Survey 7 (Attribute Conformance)

Name of the Financial Institution Your Bank	Describes The Bank Perfectly	Very Well	Fairly Well	Slightly	Doesn't Describe It At All
Progressive	☐ 1	☐ 2	☐ 3	☐ 4	☐ 5
Reliable.	☐ 1	☐ 2	☐ 3	☐ 4	☐ 5
Approachable	☐ 1	☐ 2	☐ 3	☐ 4	☐ 5
Specialists.	☐ 1	☐ 2	☐ 3	☐ 4	☐ 5
Boastful.	☐ 1	☐ 2	☐ 3	☐ 4	☐ 5
Austere	☐ 1	☐ 2	☐ 3	☐ 4	☐ 5
Forward looking	☐ 1	☐ 2	☐ 3	☐ 4	☐ 5
Flexible	☐ 1	☐ 2	☐ 3	☐ 4	☐ 5
Knowledgeable	☐ 1	☐ 2	☐ 3	☐ 4	☐ 5
Isolated	☐ 1	☐ 2	☐ 3	☐ 4	☐ 5
Prestigious	☐ 1	☐ 2	☐ 3	☐ 4	☐ 5
Technically advanced. . .	☐ 1	☐ 2	☐ 3	☐ 4	☐ 5
Responsive	☐ 1	☐ 2	☐ 3	☐ 4	☐ 5
Unique	☐ 1	☐ 2	☐ 3	☐ 4	☐ 5
Pros	☐ 1	☐ 2	☐ 3	☐ 4	☐ 5
Modern	☐ 1	☐ 2	☐ 3	☐ 4	☐ 5
Outgoing	☐ 1	☐ 2	☐ 3	☐ 4	☐ 5
Bullish	☐ 1	☐ 2	☐ 3	☐ 4	☐ 5
Cold	☐ 1	☐ 2	☐ 3	☐ 4	☐ 5
Friendly.	☐ 1	☐ 2	☐ 3	☐ 4	☐ 5
Unlimited	☐ 1	☐ 2	☐ 3	☐ 4	☐ 5
Snobbish	☐ 1	☐ 2	☐ 3	☐ 4	☐ 5
Old-Fashioned	☐ 1	☐ 2	☐ 3	☐ 4	☐ 5
Formidable	☐ 1	☐ 2	☐ 3	☐ 4	☐ 5
Sexy	☐ 1	☐ 2	☐ 3	☐ 4	☐ 5
Pretentious	☐ 1	☐ 2	☐ 3	☐ 4	☐ 5
Attentive	☐ 1	☐ 2	☐ 3	☐ 4	☐ 5
Impersonal	☐ 1	☐ 2	☐ 3	☐ 4	☐ 5
Bureaucratic	☐ 1	☐ 2	☐ 3	☐ 4	☐ 5
Grass roots	☐ 1	☐ 2	☐ 3	☐ 4	☐ 5
Action making.	☐ 1	☐ 2	☐ 3	☐ 4	☐ 5
Scientific	☐ 1	☐ 2	☐ 3	☐ 4	☐ 5
Dominating	☐ 1	☐ 2	☐ 3	☐ 4	☐ 5
Insular	☐ 1	☐ 2	☐ 3	☐ 4	☐ 5
Resourceful	☐ 1	☐ 2	☐ 3	☐ 4	☐ 5
Traditional	☐ 1	☐ 2	☐ 3	☐ 4	☐ 5

SURVEY RESULTS
1 — How Problems Experienced in Cash Letter Vary in Frequency

Problem	Fre-quently	Occa-sionally	Seldom	Never	No Answer	Un-certain
	%	%	%	%	%	%
Funds not made available as promised	3	16	51	28	2	1
Airport courier connections missed	4	24	38	29	3	2
Differences in deposit totals	9	34	49	6	1	1
In-bank courier delivery problems	2	19	53	23	2	1
Advice of deposit inadequate	3	13	52	30	1	1
Photostat copies of checks not received	5	24	52	14	2	3
Statement not received promptly	6	24	46	18	2	4
Collection of foreign or non-par items unsatisfactory	5	21	44	20	5	5
Other	0	1	0	1	96	0

Survey Results 1

Cash letter managers seldom or never experience a problem in not receiving funds from cash letters on the availability date. Only 19% of the correspondent banks have experienced this problem.

Problems experienced are more likely to be ones involving:

      1 Differences in deposit totals
      2 Statement not received promptly
      3 Photostat copies of checks not received
      4 Airport courier connections missed.

Reprinted by permission of Greenwich Research Associates

2 — How Problems That Jeopardize Cash Letter Business Vary

Problem	Most Jeopardize	Least Jeopardize	Difference
	%	%	
Funds not made available as promised	62	0	62
Airport courier connections missed	13	13	0
Differences in deposit totals	11	3	8
In-bank courier delivery problems	5	8	−3
Advice of deposit inadequate	3	6	−3
Photostat copies of checks not received	2	10	−8
Statement not received promptly	2	28	−26
Collection of foreign or non-par items unsatisfactory	1	22	−21
Other	0	1	−1
None	1	2	
No Answer	16	17	
Uncertain	3	4	

Survey Results 2

Not receiving funds from cash letter collections would jeopardize relationships significantly *more* than other cash letter problems.

Two problems are *least* to jeopardize cash letter relationships:

       1 Statement not received promptly
       2 Collection of foreign or non-par items unsatisfactory.

Reprinted by permission of Greenwich Research Associates

3 — How Problems Experienced in Wire Transfer Vary in Frequency

Problem	Fre- quently	Occa- sionally	Seldom	Never	No Answer	Un- certain
	%	%	%	%	%	%
Incorrect amount transferred	1	16	67	13	2	1
Too slow in making transfers	8	41	40	8	2	1
Transfer sent to wrong bank	1	26	57	13	2	0
Specific instructions not followed	3	26	58	10	2	0
Amount of transfer not credited/debited to right account	3	29	58	7	2	1
Too slow in advising of completed transfer	22	38	29	7	3	1
Incorrect advice of transfer	3	18	66	11	2	0
Too slow in correcting errors	18	39	33	7	3	1

Survey Results 3

Two problems experienced most *frequently* by wire transfer managers are:

1 Too slow in correcting errors
2 Too slow in advising of completed transfer.

Being too slow in correcting errors ranks as one of the most important problems that jeopardize a relationship. Only 10% of the wire transfer managers say that being slow in advising of completed transfer jeopardizes a correspondent relationship.

Reprinted by permission of Greenwich Research Associates

4 — How Problems That Jeopardize Wire Transfer Relationships Vary

Problem	Most Jeopardize	Least Jeopardize	Difference
	%	%	
Incorrect amount transferred	26	1	25
Too slow in making transfers	22	6	16
Transfer sent to wrong bank	16	2	14
Specific instructions not followed	14	6	8
Amount of transfer not credited/debited to right account	12	5	7
Too slow in advising of completed transfer	6	26	−20
Incorrect advice of transfer	3	13	−10
Too slow in correcting errors	15	14	1
Other	1	2	−1
None	1	8	
No Answer	18	19	
Uncertain	2	4	

Survey Results 4

Two problems would *most* jeopardize a wire transfer relationship for the wire transfer department managers:

1 Incorrect amount transferred
2 Too slow in making transfers.

To problems are *least* likely to jeopardize a wire transfer relationship:

1 Too slow in advising of completed transfer
2 Incorrect advice of transfer.

Reprinted by permission of Greenwich Research Associates

BIBLIOGRAPHY

Adams, E.E., Jr., J.C. Hershauer, and W.A. Ruch, *Measuring the Quality Dimension of Service Productivity,* National Science Foundation Grant, April 76-07140.

American Insurance Company, *Quality Improvement Techniques,* New York: American Management Association, 1962.

American Society for Quality Control. *Quality Costs—What & How,* 2nd edition. Milwaukee, Wisconsin, 1971.

American Society for Quality Control, *Quality Motivation Workbook,* Milwaukee, Wisconsin, 1967.

D.N. Amsden and R.T. Amsden, eds., *QC Circles: Applications, Tools, and Theory,* (Milwaukee, Wisconsin: American Society for Quality Control, 1976).

Anderson, V.N. "Five Steps to Quality Control of Clerical Operations," *Systems and Procedures Journal,* November and December 1964, pp. 8-12.

Aubrey, Charles A. II, Eldridge, Lawrence A., "Stressing Quality—The Path to Productivity," *The Magazine of Bank Administration,* (June, 1983), pp. 20-24.

Aubrey, Charles A. II, "Using Quality Circles In Banking," *Enterprising Ideas,* Vol. I, Issue II 1982), pp. 11-12.

Aubrey, Charles A. II, "Continental Quality Circles: The Circle Approach in a Service Industry," *Quality Circle Digest,* (August, 1982), pp. 55-59.

Aubrey, Charles A. II, Eldridge, Lawrence A., "Banking on High Quality," *Quality Progress,* (December, 1981), pp. 14-19.

Aubrey, Charles A. II, Zimbler, Debra A., "The Banking Industry: Quality Costs and Improvement," *Quality Progress,* (December 1983), pp. 16-20.

Aubrey, Charles A. II, Zimbler, Debra A., "Quality + or − Quality Costs Equals Productivity," *37th Annual Quality Congress Transactions,* (May, 1983)

Aubrey, Charles A. II, Hirsch, Laurie A., "Implementation, Operation and Results of Bank Circles," *3rd Annual International Association of Quality Circles Conference Transactions,* (April, 1983)

Aubrey, Charles A. II, Fencl, Wendy C., "Management Professional and Clerical Quality Circles," *36th Annual Quality Congress Transactions,* (May, 1982)

Aubrey, Charles A. II, Zimbler, Debra A., "A Banking Quality Cost Model, Its Uses and Results," *36th Annual Quality Congress Transactions,* (May, 1982)

Aubrey, Charles A. II, "Quality Circles in Banking," *The Southern Banker,* (May, 1982), pp. 30-32.

Bank Administration Manual, Park Ridge, Illinois: Bank Administration Institute—Technical Division, 1970.

Bareau, Paul, "An Outside View," Chapter 3, *The Bank of England Today,* London: Institute of Bankers, 1964.

J.F. Beardsley and D.L. Dewar, *Quality Circles,* (Cupertino, California: International Association of Quality Circles, 1978).

Benz, William M., "Quality Control in the Office," *Industrial Quality Control,* Volume 23, Number 11 (May 1967), pp. 531-534.

Berger, Roger W., "Developing Quality Information Systems," in the *Administration Application Division of the American Society for Quality Control 1976 Yearbook,* Hot Springs, Arkansas: S.G. Johnson, 1976, pp. 27-48.

Bergstrom, James, *Teller Differences Rate—A Study of Factors Affecting Teller Performance,* Publication 700 (Park Ridge, Illinois: Bank Administration Institute, 1976).

Brooks, Eliot, "A Significant Capital Market," *The Financial Times* (London), December 27, 1973, p. 13.

Brouillette, Geoff, "Wells Fargo Uses Computer to Help Respond to Queries, Track Problems," *American Banker,* February 6, 1979, p. 6.

Brown, A.W., "Professionalism—Let's Give it a New Dimension," in the *Administrative Application Division of the American Society for Quality Control 1975 Yearbook,* Milwaukee, Wisconsin, 1975, p. 20.

Caplen, Rowland, *A Practical Approach to Quality Control,* Cahners Books, 1972.

Carter, Jr., C.L., "Results and How to Get Them," in the *Administrative Application Division of the American Society for Quality Control 1976 Yearbook,* Hot Springs, Arkansas: S.G. Johnson, 1976, pp. 49-55.

"Citibank Maintains Business Faces Squeeze on Profits," *The Weekly Bond Buyer* (New York), August 20, 1973, p. 3.

Cole, R.E., *Diffusion of New Work Structures in Japan,* (University of Michigan, presented before the First Annual International Conference on Quality Circles, San Francisco, February 15-16, 1979).

Cole, R.E., *Work Mobility and Participation: A Comparative Study of American and Japanese Industry,* (University of Michigan, published by University of California Press, 1979).

Corns, M.C., *The Practical Operations and Management of a Bank,* 2d edition, Boston, Massachusetts: Bankers Publishing Company, 1968.

Crosby, Philip B., *Cutting the Cost of Quality,* Boston, Massachusetts: Industrial Education Institute, 1967.

Crosby, Philip B., *Quality is Free: The Art of Making Quality Certain,* McGraw-Hill Book Company, 1979.

Dawes, Edgar W., "Optimizing Attribute Sampling Cost," in *Twenty-Seventh Annual Technical Conference Transactions,* Milwaukee: American Society for Quality Control, 1973, pp. 181-187.

Day, Carl A., "What Can Management Expect from Quality Control," in *Quality Control in Action,* Report number 9, American Management Association, 1958, p. 17.

Deming, William Edwards, *Some Theory of Sampling,* New York: John Wiley & Sons, 1950.

Deming, William Edwards, *Elementary Principles of the Statistical Control of Quality,* 2d edition, Tokyo, Japan: Nippon Kagaku Gijutsu Remmei, 1952.

Deming, W. Edwards, "My View of Quality Control in Japan," *Reports of Statistical Application Research, Union of Japanese Scientists and Engineers,* Volume 22, Number 2 (June 1975) pp. 7-80.

Deming, W. Edwards, "Some Statistical Logic in the Management of Quality," in *All India Conference on Quality Control Proceedings,* New Delhi, May 1971, pp. 98ff.

Dertinger, E.F., "Quality Assurance: A New Organizational Concept." in the *New Concepts in Manufacturing Management,* New York: American Management Association, Inc., 1961, pp. 50-55.

Dun and Bradstreet, Inc., "Pittsburgh Area Middle Market Banking Study," September 1978, pp. 1-5.

Evans, Gordon H., "Manufacturing Staff Services," in Managerial Job Descriptions in Manufacturing, New York: American Management Association, Inc., 1964, pp. 249-280.

Exton, Jr. William, "How to Improve Clerical Accuracy," *Supervisory Management,* April 1971, p. 30 (Condensed from *Personnel Journal, Inc.,* Volume 49, Number 8, 1970).

Exton, Jr. William, "How error-prone is your bank?", *Banking,* May, 1977.

Feigenbaum, Armond V., "Total Quality Control," in *Quality Control in Action,* Report Number 9, New York: American Management Association, p. 35.

Feigenbaum, A.V., *Total Quality Control: Engineering and Management,* McGraw-Hill Book Company, Inc., 1961.

Feigenbaum, A.V., *Total Quality Control Engineering and Management,* Revision originally published title: *Quality Control,* New York: McGraw-Hill, 1961.

Fetter, Robert B., *The Quality Control System,* Homewood, Illinois: Richard D. Irwin, 1967.

Golomski, William A., "Are You Selling Quality Short?", *Nation's Business,* December 1967, pp. 72-74.

Golomski, William A., "Quality Control—History in the Making," *Quality Progress,* Volume 9, Number 7 (July 1976), pp. 16-18.

Groocock, J.M., *The Cost of Quality,* New York: Pitnam Publishing, 1974.

"Group Interviews—Sound Way to Pretest New Service Marketability," *Savings Bank Journal,* December 1973, pp. 55-57.

Gryna, Jr. Frank M., "User Quality Costs," *Quality Progress,* Volume V, Number II (November 1972), p. 18.

Hagan, John T., *A Management Role for Quality Control,* New York: American Management Association, Inc., 1968.

Hicks, Kenneth, "FN Ore. May Reopen Information Hotline To Promote Products," *American Banker,* September 18, 1979, p. 8.

Hubbard and Associates, Inc., "Chicago Loop Shopping Survey," October 1978, pp. 1-5.

Hubbard, James, "Primary Research Interviewing Techniques," *Bank Marketing,* July 1978, pp. 40-53.

Hutnyan, Joseph D., "Banks Urged to Profit from Airlines in Using Customer Feedback as Tool," *American Banker,* pp. 8-11.

International Association of Quality Circles Quarterly Reports, Second Quarter, Third Quarter, 1978, Fourth Quarter, 1978.

Ishikawa, Dr. Kaoru, *Guide to Quality Control,* (Tokyo, Japan: Asian Productivity Organization, 1976).

Juran, J.M., *Quality Control Handbook,* McGraw-Hill, New York, Third Edition, 1974.

Juran, J.M., and Gryna, F.M., *Quality Planning and Analysis From Product Development through Use,* McGraw-Hill, New York, 1980.

Juran, Joseph M. "Identifying and Solving the Company's Major Quality Problems," in *Quality Control in Action,* Report Number 9, New York: American Management Association, p. 27.

Juran, J.M., *Industrial Quality Control: The QC Circle Phenomenon* (ASQC, Industrial Quality Control, January, 1967), Volume 23, No. 7, pp. 239-336.

Juran, J.M., "Quality Control of Service—The 1974 Japanese Symposium," *Quality Progress,* Volume 8, Number 4 (April 1975), pp. 10-13.

Kelly, Dr. Patrick J., "Using the Semantic Differential," Bank Marketing, September 1973, pp. 25-28.

Kirby, E., "Quality Control in Banking," in *Administrative Application Division of the American Society for Quality Control 1975 Yearbook,* Hot Springs, Arkansas: S.G. Johnson, 1976, pp. 62-72.

Kirkpatrick, Elwood G., *Quality Control for Managers and Engineers,* John Wiley & Sons, 1970.

Langevin, Roger G., "General Quality Control Model for Bank Operations," in *Twenty-Fifth Annual Conference on Quality Control,* (New York: Rutgers University, September 8, 1973).

Langevin, Roger G., *Quality Control in the Service Industries,* Management Briefing, American Management Associations, 1977.

Latzko, William J., "A Quality Control System for Banks," *The Magazine of Bank Administration,* November 1972, pp. 17-23.

Latzko, William J., "Quality Control for Banks," *The Bankers Magazine,* Volume 160, Number 4 (Autumn 1977).

Latzko, William J., "Why Banks Need Bullseye Accuracy and Consistency," *Printing Impressions,* Volume 20, Number 7 (December 1977) pp. 100-105.

Latzko, William J., "Quality Control in Banking," *National Operations and Automation Conference Proceedings,* (New York: American Bankers Association, 1974), pp. 36-49.

Latzko, William J., "Reducing Clerical Quality Costs," in *Twenty-Eighth Annual Technical Conference Proceedings,* (Boston: American Society for Quality Control, 1974), pp. 185ff.

Latzko, William J., "QUIP—The Quality Improvement Program," in *Twenty-Ninth Annual Technical Conference Proceedings,* (San Diego: American Society for Quality Control, 1975), pp. 246ff.

Latzko, William J., "Basic Tools for Clerical Quality Control," in *Twenty-Seventh Annual Conference Proceedings,* (New Brunswick: Metropolitan Section, American Society for Quality Control, 1968) pp. 27ff.

Latzko, William J., "Quality Control in Banking," in *Twenty-Fourth Annual Conference Proceedings,* (New Brunswick: Metropolitan Section, American Society for Quality Control, 1972), pp. 61ff.

Latzko, William J., "Clerical Process Capability," in *Twenty-Fifth Annual Conference Proceedings,* (New Brunswick: Metropolitan Section, American Society for Quality Control, 1972), pp. 131ff.

Lefevre, H.L., "Budgeting Time," in *Administrative Application Division of the American Society for Quality Control 1975 Yearbook,* Milwaukee, Wisconsin, 1975, p. t.

Lester, Ronald H., et al., *Quality Control for Profit,* Industrial Press, Inc., 1978.

Lieberman, William L., "Organization and Administration of a Quality Control Program," *Industrial Quality Control,* January 1962, pp. 27-30.

Litzenberger, R.H., "The Effect of Credit on the Transaction Demand for Cash," *Journal of Finance,* Volume 26 (December 1971).

MacBryde, Vernon, "Controlling the Cost of Quality," in *Administrative Application Division of the American Society for Quality Control 1976 Yearbook,* Hot Springs, Virginia: S.G. Johnson, 1976, pp. 20-26.

MacCrehan, William A., Jr., "Cost Considerations in Planning a Quality Control Program," in Quality Control in Action, Report Number 9, New York: American Management Association, Inc., p. 48.

McConnell, Richard, "Focus on Washington: SEC Requires Disclosures of Compensating Balances," *Banking, Journal of the American Bankers Association,* Volume 66 (December 1973), p. 8.

Mears, Peter, "An Empirical Investigation of Banking Customers' Perception of Bank Machines," *Journal of Bank Research,* Summer 1978, pp. 112-115.

Mills, Ted, *Europe's Industrial Democracy: An American Response,* (Harvard Business Review, November-December, 1978), pp. 143-152.

Murdock, Bennett B., "Quality Control in Clerical Operations," in *Leadership in the Office,* New York: American Management Association, Inc., 1963, pp. 243-247.

Nadler, Paul S., "A Look at the Future of American Banking," in Prochnow, Herbert V., and Prochnow, Herbert V., Jr., (Editors), *The Changing World of Banking,* New York: Harper & Row, 1974, pp. 385-386.

"New Action Line Form Solicits More Customer Input," *Banker,* March 1980, p. 2.

Niland, Powell, *The Quality Control Circle: An Analysis,* (Singapore: McGraw-Hill Far Eastern Publishers (S) Ltd., 1971).

Nixon, Frank, *Managing to Achieve Quality and Reliability,* McGraw-Hill Book Company, 1971.

Olmstead, Blair E., "Quality Control Applied to Clerical Operations," in *Twenty-Second Annual Conference,* New Brunswick: American Society for Quality Control, September 12, 1970).

Ott, Ellis R., *Process Quality Control,* New York: McGraw-Hill Book Company, 1975.

Peat, Marwick, Mitchell & Co., *Quality Controls Accounting and Auditing,* New York, 1976.

Pratt, Robert W., Jr., "Understanding the Decision Process for Consumer Durable Goods," in Peter D. Bennett (Editor), *Marketing and Economic Development,* Chicago: American Marketing Association, 1965.

Prevete, Joan, "Citibank's Trace System Helps Cut Reject Volume in Half," *Bank Systems and Equipment,* May 1975, pp. 38-39.

Price, Waterhouse & Co., *Quality Control in a Large Professional Practice,* 2d edition, New York, 1975.

Publisher of Japan: *Quality Control Circle Case Studies,* (Japan: Asian Productivity Organization, 1972).

Quality Costs Technical Committee, ASQC, Guide For Reducing Quality Costs, American Society For Quality Control, Milwaukee, Wisconsin, 1977.

Richman, Alan, "Bankers Trust Combats Rejects With Strong Prevention Program," *Bank Systems and Equipment,* September 1975, pp. 54-57.

Rosander, A.C., "A Case Study in Controlling Quality & Products of a Large Nationwide Sample of Railroad Freight Traffic," in *Administrative Application Division of the American Society for Quality Control 1975 Yearbook,* Milwaukee, Wisconsin, 1975, p. 42.

Schaffir, Walter B., "Developing a Management Control 'Instrument Panel': A Practical Approach," in *Men, Machines and Methods in the Modern Office,* Report Number 6, New York: American Management Association, 1958, p. 61.

Sheldon, George W., and Frederick E. Finch, "Bank Queues: A Comparative Analysis of Waiting Lines," *Magazine of Bank Administration,* July 1976, pp. 31-35.

Shewhart, W.A., *Economic Control of Quality of Manufactured Product,* Princeton, New Jersey: D. van Nostrand Company, 1931.

Sills, Budd, "Making Quality Control Work in the Office," in *Men, Machines and Methods in the Modern Office,* Report Number 6, New York: American Management Association, 1958, p. 72.

Simmons, David A., *Practical Quality Control,* Reading, Massachusetts: Addison-Wesley, 1970.

Smith, Martin R., *Qualitysense: Organizational Approaches to Improving Product Quality and Service,* American Management Associations, 1979.

Staab, Thomas C., "Quality Applicable to Paperwork?—Probably!," in *Twenty-Seventh Annual Technical Transaction,* (Milwaukee: American Society for Quality Control, 1973), pp. 393-397.

Stafeil, Walter W., *1974 Survey of the Check Collection System,* Park Ridge, Illinois: Bank Administration Institute, 1975.

Stafeil, Walter W., "Exception Item 'Horror Story' May Yet Have a Happy Ending," *American Banker,* May 16, 1977.

"The Status of Interchange Plans for Cash Dispensers and Automated Tellers," *The Magazine of Bank Administration,* Volume 49 (October 1973), p. 68.

Trapp, Brian E., "The Building of an Effective MICR Quality Control Program," in *Twenty-Ninth Annual Technical Conference Proceedings,* (San Diego: American Society for Quality Control, 1975), pp. 255ff.

Van Horne, James C., *Financial Management and Policy,* 2d edition, Englewood Cliffs, New Jersey: Prentice Hall, 1971.